SELF-ESTEEM
for Children

A parent's gift that lasts forever

Dale R. Olen, Ph.D.

A Life Skills Parenting Book
JODA Communications, Ltd.
Milwaukee, Wisconsin

Editor: Chris Roerden
Design & Layout: Chris Roerden & Associates
Copyright 1996 by Dale R.Olen, Ph.D.
All rights reserved

Published by: JODA Communications, Ltd.
10125 West North Avenue
Milwaukee, WI 53226

PRINTED IN THE UNITED STATES OF AMERICA

Publisher's Cataloging in Publication

Olen, Dale R.
    Self-esteem for children: a parent's gift that lasts forever /
by Dale R. Olen.
        p. cm. — (Life skills parenting series; no. 3)
        Includes index.
        ISBN 1-56583-016-4.

    1. Self-esteem in children. 2. Parenting. 3. Child psychol-
ogy.
I. Title. II. Series.

BF723.S3054 1996   155.2'32

CH 9/97

Table of Contents

Introduction

Write out your hopes and goals for your child. What do you wish for her by the time she's 18? I'll bet that near the top of your list you'll find a statement like one of these:

"That she really likes herself."

"That she feels confident and self-assured."

"That she is comfortable with who she is."

Parents have an instinctive sense that self-esteem is the bedrock of personal growth. And they're right. You know that developing a sense of responsibility, becoming intellectually independent, learning to love and care about others—all are based on a strong and positive acceptance of self. You know that children who don't value themselves show a lack of self-confidence, fail to get involved in school and life activities, become too dependent on what others think and often end up as underachievers.

So a child's self-esteem stands out as a primary goal in your work as a parent. It's why you picked up this book. It's central for me as well. My two children are pretty well raised, although I guess I'll always do some "raising" no matter how old they are. I still believe their sense of self is the most important characteristic they possess. If they have positive self-esteem, they'll do just fine.

Over the years I've seen their self-esteem rise and fall for many reasons. When my daughter, Amy, was a youngster, her self-esteem and a yo-yo had a lot in common. We were never quite sure how she was feeling about herself. My wife would have to ask: "Amy, on a scale from one to ten, with one being absolutely no self-esteem and ten being super-high self-esteem, where are you now?" And Amy would give her a number. Often we'd be surprised. When we'd think it was at two, Amy would say eight. That was always good to hear. It was harder to hear when she said two or three.

My experience with my children, as well as with all the children I've seen in therapy over the years, tells me that self-esteem is extremely fluid early in life. Children's self-concept floats like a tiny fishing boat adrift in the ocean. On calm, windless days, the boat glides gently through the waters, acting just the way a boat ought to act. But on stormy days, the boat gets tossed and thrown about and makes no headway at all. In fact, it simply tries to survive the wash of the waves and the violent winds.

Children's self-esteem is largely determined by the forces that touch, push and pull them, bombard them and support them. At first their self-esteem is shaped and formed by what happens outside of them. Since they can't control all the outside forces that touch them, their self-esteem is sometimes pummeled to the ground and at other times raised to the stars. It seems as if self-esteem lies beyond their control.

There's a good reason for this: Throughout the first half of our lives we focus on the external world. Our entire orientation is outside ourselves. Young children, especially, spend all their time trying to figure out how to navigate in this world. They attempt to fit in, make the world work for them, not get hurt, have pleasure and fun and be successful. They develop a super-sensitivity to all that's happening around them. They shape their identity based on the feedback they get and what happens to them in that outside world.

As you know, that outside world is fickle and oh so changing. One moment a classmate tells your son how smart he is and the next moment what a stupid jerk he is. One minute you, the parent, are very pleased with your daughter's cooperative behavior and the next minute you're angry with her for hitting her brother.

Initially, her identity and self-esteem are shaped and formed by your responses. She has nothing else to use in determining if she's an okay person or not. A rather fragile basis for self-worth, right? But that's the reality. Children form their self-esteem based on their experiences of the outside, changing, fickle world. No wonder you and I as parents instinctively know that what we do in relation to our children plays a vital role in their self-esteem.

This book, then, is really about you as a parent. What you do and don't do has a lot of impact on how well your children feel about themselves. I don't want to place the entire burden of your children's self-esteem on you. There are too many other forces out there influencing self-esteem. But you are significant. There are specific things you can do to help your children improve their feelings about themselves. I want to discuss those principles and tools with you here.

One point of clarification before we get started. We all use a variety of words to talk about self-esteem. I want to make sure that as you read this book our words mean the same things.

The term "self-concept" simply means the notion a child has of herself. There is no value judgment made here. Self-concept involves a description of the self. For example, "I am a third-grader. I work hard on my studies. I like basketball and playing the guitar. I am usually kind to my sister." All these descriptions are part of a young child's self-concept. Another word for self-concept is "identity."

"Self-esteem" and "self-worth" are terms that I will use interchangeably. Self-esteem can be high or low. Self-esteem involves a *judgment* about the self-concept. For example, the self-concept might say: "I work hard on my studies." Self-esteem occurs when the child judges that notion as positive or negative. She says to herself: "I work hard on my studies and that's good about me." When she judges positively, her self-worth or self-esteem is high.

Positive self-esteem can be taught. You, as the parent, play an essential role in helping your children develop this important foundational skill—the skill of feeling good about the self.

HOW SELF-ESTEEM DEVELOPS

Alan is 44 years old. He stands 5'8" tall and weighs 225 pounds. He dislikes himself intensely. He describes his inner self as a rotten, smelly and evil ball with jagged edges sitting in the pit of his stomach. He believes that he never does anything right. He wants desperately to be close to someone but is convinced "nobody could ever love me." He never married.

Alan is a very generous and kind man. He anticipates people's needs and enjoys meeting those needs. He possesses an excellent sense of humor, and people respond positively to him. His friends have no clue that Alan doesn't like himself. They like him, so they assume he likes himself too. Little do they know.

How did Alan develop such a negative view of himself? What ingredients were thrown into the mix that served up such low self-esteem? What happened to him as a youngster that now so strongly influences his life?

Psychologists offer many answers to these questions, and no single theory seems to explain the whole issue. So let me present several explanations on how self-esteem develops in childhood and how it affects Alan and the rest of us in adulthood.

Answer 1

Alan went through four mental processes in order to view himself negatively. He began this process as a child and continues it today.

When Alan was six he accidentally knocked over a flower pot and broke it. His mom reacted by yelling, "What's the matter with you, Alan? You're so clumsy. You go right to your room." Alan headed for his room, while the four mental processes clicked through his mind almost simultaneously:

1. Perception
2. Self-talk
3. Judgment
4. Reaction

First, he *perceived* or took in what had just happened. He observed the *facts* of the case. Assuming his perceptions were accurate, he noticed:

Fact: I knocked down a plant.

Fact: The pot broke and so did the plant.

Fact: A mess was created in the family room.

Fact: My mother was angry.

Fact: My mother said I was clumsy and she wondered what was the matter with me.

Fact: My mother sent me to my room.

Once Alan had these facts in his mind, he went on to mental process 2, *self-talk*. Alan discussed with himself what just happened. He thought:

"I wonder if Mom doesn't like me anymore. Maybe

I *am* a klutz. If she thinks I'm clumsy, maybe I'll never be any good in sports or anything. Maybe I'm not really clumsy, but just had an accident. Then maybe Mom is wrong about calling me clumsy."

This is self-talk. Alan considered his perceptions of reality and then raised hypotheses about what they meant. He pushed possible interpretations of the event through his mind in order to know how to respond to it.

Clearly, Alan at age six did not consciously think through all the "maybes" suggested above. His self-talk occurred in a split second. He laid out all the options available to him at the moment and quickly moved to the next process, *judgment.*

In this third process, Alan *judged* his hypotheses and decided what his perceptions of the event *meant.* The judgment process stands as the pivotal moment in positive and negative self-esteem. If he judges positively he concludes: "Mother is simply irritated with me and so uses those words. But it does not mean I *am* a clumsy and uncoordinated person. In fact, I know from being in that tennis class that I am quite coordinated."

On the other hand, if Alan judges negatively, he concludes: "She really dislikes me and that must mean I am a bad boy. I am a clumsy kid who can't do anything right."

Again, let me say that children don't think out this kind of situation in such a slow and deliberate way. The process speeds along so quickly that their self-talk and judgments elude their awareness. But even though they may not be aware of these mental processes, each one is taking place.

But, you might be asking, why do some kids make positive judgments and some, like Alan, make negative ones? The range of answers to that question is, in part, presented next. For now, however, let me say that the children who make positive judgments *experience* acceptance as individuals regularly from the significant people in their lives. Children who draw negative conclusions about themselves do not experience that unconditional acceptance from the important adults in their lives. They sense that their goodness and worth are based on a set of conditions outside themselves that they must fulfill so they can feel of value. Children who develop low self-esteem feel they can never quite measure up to those conditions and expectations. They don't perform well enough to be valued. Therefore, they conclude they are not good people.

These young children often learn to make critical judgments that cause difficulty for them in later life. They learn to believe such things as:
- I am a good person only when I please my parents.
- I am a good person when I am successful.
- If I make a mistake, I am a failure.
- If I don't accomplish this task or goal, it is (I am) terrible.
- If Dad or Mom is upset, it's my fault and I'm bad.

- I should excel in this sport; if I don't I'm inadequate.
- If you don't pay attention to me, then I don't count.

This type of thinking, developed early in children's lives, plays havoc with self-esteem. The conclusions or judgments children make that lead to negative self-concepts fall into three categories:

1. Dramatic judgments:

- It's awful.
- Mom will never like me again.
- I can't stand it in this house. They don't care.
- They must think I'm terrible.
- I can't do anything right.

2. Demand judgments:

- I must get straight A's on my report card.
- I have to have a date for the prom.
- I must make the team or I'll die.
- I absolutely need that bike.
- I have to get them to like me.

3. Self-blame or inclusive judgments:

- I got a B on my report card, therefore I'm dumb.
- I have acne, therefore I'm ugly.
- I'm afraid to ride the roller coaster, therefore I'm a chicken.
- No one is talking to me at this party, therefore I must be a real nerd.

You can see that self-blame judgments are the ones that ultimately sabotage a child's feelings about self. Dramatic judgments and demand judgments set the stage for a clinching self-blame statement. For example:

"I must get straight A's" (a demand thought) leads to "if I don't I'm dumb" (self-blame judgment).

"I have to make the team" (demand thought) and "if I don't I'll die" (dramatic thought) lead to "I probably won't make the team because I'm no good anyway" (self-blame).

The last part of each of these dramatic and demanding thoughts carries the negative, destructive judgment about the self.

Remember Alan? He *perceives* a situation, he *talks to himself* about it, and he *judges* himself and the situation in dramatic and demanding fashion. In the fourth and final process of the self-esteem journey, Alan *reacts* to his negative self-judgment with feelings and behaviors. He concludes that he is inadequate as a person, so his feeling reaction is depression. His behavior is to withdraw from people and keep his deepest thoughts to himself.

Let's leave Alan now and take a look at 12-year-old Beth. This young woman walks through the first three processes—perception, self-talk and judgment—coming to the conclusion that she will never be successful at anything she does. When cheerleading tryouts begin, her *reactions,* based on her self-judgment are these:

Behavior: She sits at home and doesn't even try out.

Feeling: She feels sad because she's left out again.

Of course, sitting at home and feeling left out reinforce a low self-concept, and the mental process begins again. Beth *perceives* herself as sitting home alone. She *talks to herself* about the possible meanings of such a situation. She *judges* herself as someone without friends and without a life. And she *reacts* by brooding even more.

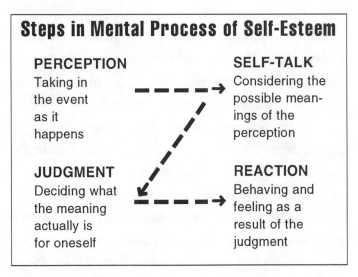

Steps in Mental Process of Self-Esteem

PERCEPTION
Taking in the event as it happens

SELF-TALK
Considering the possible meanings of the perception

JUDGMENT
Deciding what the meaning actually is for oneself

REACTION
Behaving and feeling as a result of the judgment

The critical step in this process is the child's *judgment*—what a child decides an event means for him or her. Any work you do in helping your child value him or herself must attack the child's judgments about self. Ways of doing this are coming in the next section.

Answer 2

Remember the questions? How did Alan develop such low self-esteem? Did anything happen to him in childhood that influenced his sense of self today? A second approach to answering those questions comes from the theory of transactional analysis developed by

Eric Berne (*Games People Play,* Grove Press, N.Y.,
1964). He's the man who first said, "I'm okay, you're
okay." Applying Berne's approach to Alan, we would
say that at birth Alan immediately assumes a psychological position. He experiences himself as helpless and
without any power to direct his own life. He senses his
parents as all-powerful and the source of all that leads to
his happiness—food, warmth, protection, love. He concludes, in a very primitive manner, that his parents are
strong and capable of all things. They are *okay*. Since he
is not strong and capable of taking care of himself, he sees
himself as *not okay*. He views himself in relation to the
world as less than or as inferior to other people.

Rooted in him now is the *experience,* not just the
judgment, of his own inadequacy. This is what Alan's
parents, and you, start with in terms of your child's
earliest experience with self-esteem. Your child seems to
start life skewed toward a negative sense of self because
he or she begins in a powerless, helpless position. He or
she is one-down, not okay.

This position is called "I'm not okay; you are okay."
Here lies the soil in which the seeds of negative self-
esteem are first sown. If Alan's earliest experience—
"I'm not okay"—continues, the belief that he is not okay
and that his parents *are* okay intensifies and spreads to all
his interpersonal experiences. In all relationships Alan
then feels "I'm not okay, and the rest of them are okay."

Thus, your child starts out in the position of "I'm not

okay." Of course, your child is not conscious of being "not okay." He or she simply starts out in a one-down position.

The way you respond to your newborn child determines whether or not she continues to believe "I'm not okay." If you are overly protective, you tell your daughter that she can't do anything on her own. Such a child can become fearful of trying new things because she believes she can't do it right without Dad or Mom helping out.

If you tend to rescue your child from frustrations, again you reinforce his belief that he is incapable of doing anything without parental help. He continues to believe "You're okay, but I'm not."

Another way in which your child can remain stuck in "I'm not okay, you are okay" occurs when you criticize your child rather than her *behavior*. Saying "Bad girl" or "How dumb can you be?" when Jennifer pushes her hand through the screened door teaches her that she *is* bad or dumb. She is not okay. You, on the other hand, must be okay, because you're judging her as less than yourself.

When you're critical of your child, you take a one-up position to her. You know what that makes her—one-down.

Around age seven months, some children begin to develop a variation on this theme. When children begin creeping and moving around on their own, they open up the possibility of a second and more difficult psychological position: "I'm not okay and neither are you okay."

With creeping, your daughter experiences some independence and some power. She can do something for
herself—not much yet, but she no longer totally depends
on you. Of course, she still needs her parents desperately.
But some parents take their daughter's first step toward
independence as their own movement toward parental
freedom. Now that their daughter can creep, these parents mistakenly think they don't need to care for her as
much. So they don't spend as much time with her. They
might not hold her as much, read to her as often, stroke
her as frequently or talk to her as intensely. This little girl
fails to get her daily dose of loving attention.

Perhaps she comes from a large family, where she's
the fourth of six children. Easily, she can get lost in the
shuffle, failing again to get the attention she needs to feel
good about herself. Perhaps she comes from a small
family of one of two children, in which the parents are
more interested in careers, friends, money and their own
recreation. In both these situations, the child gets lost,
feels abandoned and comes to the conclusion: "I'm not
okay, but neither are they okay." The adults have let this
child down.

You can see the havoc that this psychological position plays with the child. Not only is Jennifer "not okay,"
but now her parents, who were so powerful, wonderful
and good, are "not okay" either. From her perspective,
her "parents" include *all* people. No one is "okay."
Everybody has a "not" in front of his or her identity. No

one out there is good for Jennifer.

As you can see, this position holds a great deal of pessimism and futility for a child. She sees herself as not capable or good, but neither can she rely on the goodness and strength of others. No one, she believes, is there for her. While she, herself, can't solve many of life's problems, she certainly cannot depend on anyone else doing so either. In the most severe case of this psychological position, the result is suicide. Feeling no power from within and finding no power from without, this person lives in despair and helplessness, concluding that the only way to handle her life is to end it.

Short of actual suicide are all the little deaths the Jennifers of the world inflict upon themselves. Because they don't believe in themselves or in others, they become shy, withdrawn, isolated. They leave reality by living in a fantasy world where they have power and control. They feel like victims, put upon at every turn. They don't take risks; they don't sing at the top of their voices; they don't dance on tables. They don't reach for the stars. They slowly die, day by day, from early childhood to the moment they are placed in the coffin. "I'm not okay, and you're not okay either" is a sad and dismal way for a child to become an adult.

A third psychological position can occur early in a child's life. This position is equally as traumatic and painful as the one just described. It happens when a child is not simply *abandoned* as described with Jennifer, but is actively *abused.* When a child is hurt repeatedly by emotional or physical attacks, he begins to wall himself in, setting up protective shields from the abuse. He knows clearly that "*they* are not okay." In fact, they are bad and must be avoided at all costs. Life is not good when they are around because they can and do hurt the child.

This young person realizes that the only time he is safe, that things are okay, is when he is alone, settled in his crib, the light off and his parents closing the door behind them as they leave his room. His experience is: "When they are around it is not okay. When I am alone it is okay—or I am okay." The child is safe and okay when he is placed in his crib and no longer needs to endure the violence of the parents. The violence may be physical, or it may be a more subtle but just as debilitating emotional violence. In emotional abuse, parents often deny they are doing anything wrong. They say things such as, "He needs to shape up and that's the way to do it," or "You have to keep kids in their place."

Emotional abuse also happens when parents don't want their children. Perhaps the pregnancy was a "surprise." The couple already has four children and cannot afford or handle a fifth. The child is unwanted and experiences as much in indirect and subtle ways.

Emotional abuse also takes place in some blended families. When a man and woman marry, perhaps she has two young children and he has already raised three. He doesn't want to deal with kids any more, but accepts them as part of the package in marrying again. But once in the family system, he ignores the children. They feel the rejection.

Sometimes the mom can also be rejecting of the kids. For example, if she sees that the children are causing tension and distance between her and her new husband, she might become angry and hostile toward the children for interfering in her adult happiness. She then takes it out on the children.

In situations where there is physical or emotional abuse, the child can grow up believing: "I'm okay, you're not okay."

Even though it appears that such a child has positive self-esteem by thinking "I'm okay...," he actually hates himself as well as the world around him. He may look strong and self-possessed, sometimes even arrogant and flamboyant. But that's usually a cover for a very inadequate sense of self underneath. He hasn't received positive feedback in his life to shore up a strong self-image. He's actually a pretty fragile young man, who camouflages it by acting cool, tough or suave.

As an adult, this young man may use people for his own purposes. He might act in a self-centered way, taking care of Number One. He may manipulate the world around him to gain his own ends. Pushing this personal style to its worst conclusion, this person can become a criminal and ultimately a murderer. He thinks: "The other person is bad and will hurt me. So I should hurt him before he hurts me."

In this psychological state—"I'm okay, but you're not okay"—the person may kill the other, whereas in the second psychological state discussed earlier—"I'm not okay, you are okay"—the person kills himself.

The fourth possible position for a child is, "I'm okay, you're okay." This is the position of choice for your child. If the child is loved from the beginning in an unconditional way by *both* parents, if both are there, then the child has a chance to gain a sense of being "okay." When your child experiences unconditional love and a gradual sense of independence and freedom, she begins to move from the birth position of "I'm *not* okay, you are okay" to "Hey, maybe I'm not so powerless myself. Maybe I'm okay too." Thus begins your child's movement into positive self-esteem.

Not only does she learn she's okay because she is well loved and able to take some power in her little world, but also she experiences you, her parents, as okay too. She sees you loving her, protecting her, supporting and encouraging her. She doesn't grow afraid of you and, consequently, doesn't fear the outside world. You *are* her outside world, and you're okay!

You want your infant child to gradually like herself and to continue liking you and other people. You want her to grow into the psychological state of "Hey, world, I'm okay. And you know what? You're okay too." You do that best by dearly loving your daughter without expecting her to be a certain wonderful way. Just love her as she is. And empower her. Give her some room to grow, to take charge of her own little world, to feel powerful.

But don't abandon her in the process. There is a fine line between letting her take charge of her world and ignoring or absenting yourself from her. Be there, loving and encouraging, but let her do what she can for herself. You give your child a great gift when you encourage her to say and believe: "I'm really okay, and so are you."

Answer 3

In our culture, self-esteem and a sense of meaning in life are closely linked. If you have a purpose for living, for getting up in the morning, then you have positive self-esteem. You develop that sense of meaning based on three pillars or sources. You may look to your *work*—or the productive use of your time—for meaning. You may center on your *interpersonal relations* for meaning. Or you might turn to God or some *transcendent purpose* to discover meaning.

MEANING AND PURPOSE IN LIFE		
WORK	RELATIONSHIPS	GOD OR HIGHER POWER

If during your lifetime one or more of these pillars is shaken or broken down, your sense of meaning and your self-esteem are going to be severely tested. A man loses his job and the important pillar of work crumbles from under him. If he has placed much of his sense of worth on his work, you can see the problem that arises. The same is true of the man or woman who loses a most significant relationship by reason of death, divorce or break-up in friendship. These are critical times in a person's life and the stuff of adult and "mid-life crises."

When you over-focus on any one of these pillars, you're steering toward trouble. If you base your esteem and value so fully on work that the other pillars suffer, you're heading for rough waters when your work is taken from you by poor health, age or boredom. If you place your entire sense of worth as a mother on your relationships, you will struggle with self-esteem when your children grow up and leave home. If you center too fully on God or a higher power as the only significant aspect of your life, you may find that when the emotional response to God wanes, so does your sense of worth and meaning.

The point of all this "adult" discussion is that these pillars are developed in childhood as the child learns to value certain things as important. For example, Steve might come to believe that "winning is everything." If he wins in Candyland as a three-year-old he feels good; if he loses he storms and feels awful. Later, he doesn't mind playing a little dirty to win at basketball or cheating to win more marbles. When he wins or otherwise succeeds, his parents rave about him and praise him; when he loses they seem more crushed than he is. This boy is learning to build up his pillar of *work* as the source of his worth as a person.

Our society reinforces the child's belief that doing things successfully makes one worthwhile. Oftentimes in therapy and in psychological testing the first question I ask someone is "Who are you?" About 80 percent of the time, the first answer I'm given is, "I am a salesman" or "a mother" or "a student." People tell me what they *do* when I ask who they *are*.

"Achieve, be successful, win"—these are the passwords in American society reinforcing the belief that "my value is based on what I *do*." Self-worth then becomes based on status—a man who is a physician has more value than an electrician, and a woman who is an executive has more worth than a "housewife."

In childhood, it's easy to believe that the captain of the cheerleaders has "more value than" the flute player in the band, and the A student is "better than" the C student.

Jimmy hits a home run and a parent says "good boy." Achievement equals goodness. Jenny washes the car and Dad says "you're really a wonderful kid." Doing and being are married in the child's mind. Children are set up for a Humpty Dumpty fall in later life when their jobs or positions are taken away or they fail to succeed at a challenging task. Their self-esteem crashes because they have not achieved.

The same can happen if a child learns that "I am worthwhile only if others need me, or like me, or are with me." Teenagers often express to me their conclusion that "the most popular kids are better than I am." Somehow *having* relationships means *being* better.

The difficulty here lies in a child's belief that "I am okay when others are valuing me or attending to me." If a child places too much emphasis on this pillar, then when he or she is alone or has experienced some rejection, the child goes to pieces. "Life is no longer worth living," which translates to "I am no longer worthwhile."

Finally, the pillar of God can be focused upon too exclusively. This rarely happens in early childhood, except in those instances where the parents or teachers claim "God's disappointment" with a child's behavior. In this ploy, parents project their own disappointment and use God to bolster their position in the argument. Teens may focus too exclusively on the God pillar for a sense of meaning and purpose. This occurs when a child's sense of stability and security is shaken in some way. The child then grabs onto the one reality he or she feels will not change or abandon him or her—a transcendent, spiritual force—God. By fully involving themselves in religion, some children discover security and meaning in life, and they experience themselves as being worthwhile—often for the first time.

Unfortunately for many of these children, the emotional high of this religious experience wanes, just as it does in a boy-girl relationship. When that happens and the teenagers no longer *feel* close to God, their self-worth may come tumbling down. At that point the best thing you can do for them is to simply *be* there. Your being there immediately affirms the pillar of relationship. Upon that pillar children can again begin to rebuild their self-worth.

Answer 4

I'd like to offer one more answer that has become increasingly important in my understanding of a child's self-esteem. It involves a very subtle belief, learned in early childhood, which operates in most adult lives.

Children learn early in life: "Two realities, if they differ, cannot stand side by side. One of them must go."

Let me explain. Sandy is six years old. She goes to bed on school nights at 8 P.M. Tonight she crawls into bed at 8 o'clock and Dad sits down to read a book. At 9 o'clock Sandy appears at the bottom of the staircase and calls "Daaaaaady." She makes an initial attempt to present to him her reality.

Dad jumps right in and says: "What are you doing up at this hour, young lady? You get up those stairs and get to sleep. It's way past your bedtime." He has presented his reality.

So Sandy has her reality and Dad has his. As we can see they are very different.

Sandy tries again, "But Daddy, I...."

Dad interrupts, "No buts about it. You have school

tomorrow and you have to get your sleep. So hustle back to bed this instant."

She goes back upstairs.

However, Sandy's reality is that she became sick and threw up in her bed. Dad's reality is his desire for her to be in bed sleeping, and for him to sit quietly and read a book. These two worlds differ. And Sandy learns a most powerful belief: "When my world differs with Dad's world (or perhaps with anybody else's world), my world doesn't count." Or, more profoundly, she learns "*I* don't count."

Think of all the times when your children's worlds might seem not to count. Your child falls and scrapes her knee. She cries and you say, "It's okay." Your world differs from hers, since clearly her scraped knee is not okay for her. Or your four-year-old keeps insisting, as mine used to, "Daddy, Daddy, Daddy," while you're talking to your partner. You say, "Joe, quiet. I'm talking to your mother." But maybe you never get back to him. He experiences his world as not counting. Or your teenager likes loud music that you don't like. You insist on quiet music. His experience? He doesn't count.

I'm not suggesting that you give in to your child's world every time it differs from your own. I am saying that through many of these experiences your child learns this subtle but powerful belief: "My world does not count when it differs from Dad and Mom's world." And some kids translate that even further to: "*I* don't count when other people differ from me."

This belief radically influences a child's self-worth in times of conflict and differences. Even if you don't agree with your child, you need to first understand his or her world. If your child's world is not understood, then the child can easily draw the conclusion: "I do not exist for them."

Two responses flow from this realization. Your child feels *hurt* and accepts the conclusion that he or she does not exist. This results in poor self-esteem. Or your child struggles harder to show Dad and Mom that he or she does in fact exist. The child then reacts with *anger* and yells back, demanding, in effect, that you pay attention and notice that he or she really does exist.

Your child's anger is almost always an effective way of getting you to deal with him or her. Anger helps the child feel as though he or she exists. "See, I do exist."

When my son, Andy, was five years old he hit me in the back of the head with a belt one night while I was helping my daughter get her pajamas on. With irritation I asked, "Andy, why in the world did you do that?" He immediately responded, "So you'd pay me some attention." Well, he got what he wanted.

His world and mine had differed. He wanted me to focus on him. I was focusing on my daughter, Amy. One of our realities had to change. He could have sat back and felt hurt and jealous because I wasn't involved in his world, or he could have demanded that I attend to his world, which is what he did in a rather dramatic, though inappropriate way.

You see, Andy believed that two opposing or differing worlds cannot exist side by side. One had to go. Because he feared that his world would have to go (that he wouldn't exist for me), he reacted strongly and attacked my world to force me to change and correspond to his world. He hit me in the head with a belt.

You might be wondering: "What else could kids believe when they experience two differing worlds?" Here's an alternative belief much more reasonable and sound: "Two differing worlds can, in fact, stand side by side and *both* be legitimate or valid."

Practically, both worlds cannot always operate at the same time, as when your son and you might want to watch different TV programs on the same set at the same time. But even though a decision for action must be made, it can be done in a manner that does not *invalidate* the other person's world.

How to work concretely with the dynamics of your children's self-esteem is discussed in the next section. So far I have focused only on *how* those self-concepts develop. Understanding the evolution of your children's sense of self will help you better grasp the principles and tools of helping your children grow up liking who they are.

PRINCIPLES AND TOOLS FOR DEVELOPING SELF-ESTEEM

Positive and negative self-esteem are learned. Although children are born into a one-down position of "I'm not okay, you are okay," they are quickly influenced to either remain there or move toward the position of "Hey, I'm okay and so are you." The push toward this dynamic and positive stance comes mainly from you as parent.

Throughout your child's development, his or her self-esteem rises and falls as a result of many situations. You aren't the only influence. But you're always important. What you do, what you say, how you say it, and what your own attitudes are continue to play a critical role in your child's sense of self.

In this chapter you'll find the principles and tools to teach your children how to like themselves throughout their childhood years and into their adult lives. Let's look at the principles and tools you need to teach your child positive self-esteem.

Principle 1

Create a home atmosphere of inclusion, control and openness.

Danny was 32 when I first met him. He complained of lacking confidence in his work and difficulty in relating to other people. He told me his story. An only child, he was the son of an alcoholic father and a sickly mother. Dad and Mom fought constantly. Danny retreated, hiding from the conflict and isolating himself from both parents. They had no time for him and gave him very little attention, except to criticize his behavior. The parents rarely communicated in constructive ways, since they were closed, secretive and dishonest.

Danny grew up in a home where he was not *included,* did not experience any *control* in his own life, and did not know an *open* and loving relationship. Consequently Danny felt *insignificant, inadequate* and *unliked.* Those three feelings became the pillars for his lack of self-confidence.

The fertile soil of positive self-esteem consists of three ingredients, according to Will Schutz in *The Human Element* (Jossey Bass, San Francisco, 1994):

    1. Inclusion.

    2. Control.

    3. Openness.

When these three elements "gift wrap" the family, children feel:

1. Significant.
2. Adequate and capable.
3. Liked.

Children need to feel significant. They do so when they are included. You have a choice and decision to make when you begin parenting: to make this a child-centered home or an adult-centered home. Most parents automatically slide into one of these two positions. I want to encourage you to make a conscious choice. And for your children's sake, I hope you choose to make your home child-centered.

When you place your children on center stage, they feel a profound sense of belonging. They learn quickly that they are significant and important characters in the drama of life. They don't play just a bit part. They play leading roles. Already you can see their self-esteem rising. You can make your home child-centered without losing yourself completely. This doesn't need to be an either/or proposition. "Oh, poor me. If I make my children the center, then I lose myself totally." No. Make your children leading characters, but put yourself in an important supporting role.

Parents who give themselves the leading roles and relegate their children to stagehands literally set the stage for low self-esteem in their children. Danny lived in an adult-centered home. He didn't count. Both his parents spent their time preoccupied with themselves and their destructive relationship. They ignored him, not because they didn't love him, but because their own pain kept them focused on themselves. Unfortunately for Danny, their concern with themselves led him to the fatal conclusion, "I am not an important person."

Before doing anything else regarding your child's self-esteem, sit yourself down and think hard about who is the central figure in this home. If it is not your child, then make her so. Part of the commitment of parenting lies in your willingness to sacrifice your own lead role and elevate your child to that position. I'm not talking about spoiling your child, only giving her a strong sense that she is significant and worth being "Number One."

If your child has been the central figure in the home, great. Re-commit yourself to keeping the home a child-centered environment. Remaining conscious of your commitment and sacrifice will help you during those times when you become preoccupied with your own world and concerns.

Once you have made your home child-centered and given your child a sense of inclusion and significance, then you can help your child feel adequate and capable. You achieve that feeling by allowing your child to *control* his or her own life in gradually increasing degrees. Danny felt little control in his home. He could not create a safe environment to live in. He lived under the constant threat of disruption, fights and violence. He had no way of stopping the critical attacks on him. He needed to have some ability, feel some power in protecting himself, keeping himself safe and feeling good in his relationships.

His father, in particular, criticized him regularly. He called him names, told him how inept he was, and laughed at him when he made mistakes. Danny began to feel inadequate. In later sections of this book I will talk more about helping your children feel good about themselves and what they do. For now I want you to fully recognize how important it is for your child to feel a sense of control and a sense of adequacy in his or her life. Feeling powerful gives your child a strong start toward positive self-esteem.

Finally, you want to create an *open and honest* environment for your child. This, too, takes a conscious decision on your part. Decide to talk with every member of the family in an honest and open manner. Openness in a relationship tells the other person that you value him, that you trust him and will entrust yourself to him, and that you like him. You tend to open yourself only with people you like.

Being open with your child tells him you value him enough to share yourself with him. Through honesty you show affection, approval and acceptance. Parents who are closed tend to express only negative, debilitating messages. They mask their deepest feelings, which are usually loving and caring.

Your child needs to know you like him. Open displays of affection and tenderness tell him that. In a way, "being open" means opening your heart. Let your heart speak to your child. Let the depth of love flow out of you in words and actions to fill your home and give your child the powerful sense that he is well-liked.

Before going on to the other principles in this book, first take inventory of your home atmosphere. Check to see if it contains:

- Inclusion leading to a feeling of significance;
- Control leading to a feeling of adequacy;
- Openness leading to a feeling of being liked and loved.

If your answer is "yes," reinforce your commitment to continue infusing your home with these attributes. If your home does not yet hold these important ingredients, then choose to insert them starting now.

Principle 2

**Set clear boundaries for your child
when he or she is young.**

This principle sounds as if it should be in a book on discipline. Setting boundaries means saying "no" and being strict. How can such activities by you help your child like him or herself?

Boundaries give definition to a child. When Kevin is newly born he has no sense of boundaries. He doesn't know where he ends and you begin. He is a free-flowing mass of human energy. Certainly he has the boundaries of his body, although he doesn't know it yet. But that's about it. He has no idea who he is or what all that stuff out there is. For all he knows, it's all part of him or he's part of it.

"Ego boundaries" is the technical term for what I'm talking about. An ego boundary is a psychological notion that describes the separation between the self and the rest of reality. Each of us has an ego boundary. It's the barrier that divides us from all else. Picture it as a circle around you, with you on the inside. From within that circle you say: "Everything inside this circle is me; everything outside the circle is not me." Your child can't say or think that yet. Kevin doesn't have an ego boundary.

Kevin, then, cannot define himself. Without an ego

boundary Kevin has no clue as to who he is. If I could draw a picture of Kevin's psyche as an infant it would look like this:

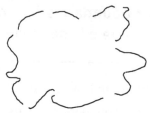

Kevin is spilling all over the place.

This is where you, the parent, come in. One of your many jobs is to help Kevin set and define his boundaries. Not right away. You can give him several months to get used to his new digs—your house, you, relatives, the world. That's a pretty big job in itself. But six or seven months into life you need to begin the job of setting boundaries.

In doing so you place limits on Kevin. You begin to draw in his amoeba-like edges. You begin to restrict his spilling over into elements of life that are "not him." The boundaries you set look like this:

You're not doing this to constrain Kevin or box him in. You're doing it to help him define himself. Why is that important for self-esteem? Because he cannot *like* himself unless he first *knows* himself. And he can't know himself without defining himself. Boundaries give him definition.

When you say "no," when you take something away from him he shouldn't have, when you pull him from the brink of the basement stairs, you are helping him define and know himself. That's the first step toward self-esteem.

As you can imagine, the way you say "no" and establish limits can lead to positive or negative self-esteem. Abusive discipline or discipline to satisfy your own needs at the expense of Kevin leads to self-knowledge, but to very negative self-esteem.

Say your "no" kindly, take away dangerous items gently and handle him with care. You need to set boundaries with love, not with power or force. In doing so, you help your child define who he is—the preamble to developing positive self-esteem.

Principle 3

**Acknowledge your child's world and
attempt to understand it.**

Children don't like to be ignored. In fact, they can't
stand it. So they work hard not to let it happen. Often their
efforts appear in the form of "misbehavior." As parents
you hear yourself saying: "Oh, she's just looking for
attention when she whines like that." Well, it's true. She
is looking for attention. She wants to be noticed. How
come?

Being noticed is the way people know they exist.
Remember René Descartes, the French philosopher, who
attempted to prove that we exist? He felt he proved it
because he experienced himself as *thinking*. Because he
thought, he figured that he must exist. He came up with
the phrase that has been heard around the world: "I think,
therefore I am."

Who knows if Descartes was correct. It's an interesting thought. Much later, another French philosopher—
this time an existentialist by the name of Gabriel Marcel—
came along and challenged Descartes' "I think, therefore
I am." Marcel said the proof that you exist is not in the fact
that you experience yourself thinking, but that you experience yourself in relationship to other people. He said
the proof of existence is not "I think, therefore I am," but

"We are, therefore I am." You know you exist when you are in relationship to other people. You need others to notice you if you are to notice yourself.

Think of a time when you said something in a group or at a meeting and no one paid attention to your words. It was as though you weren't there. Women feel this lack of attention regularly in business meetings and at home. An often-expressed complaint I hear in couple's counseling is: "He doesn't listen." "He never notices." "He doesn't compliment." "I'm not a priority in his life." By and large in our society, women have not felt as though they counted. They feel their voices have been silenced. They often experience themselves as not existing.

For the women reading this, you know what it's like not to be noticed. You know what happens to your self-esteem. You know how you begin to doubt yourself, question your validity in the world and wonder if you count in any way.

For the men reading this, you may have a little more difficulty in identifying the feelings of non-existence that arise from not being noticed. But you, too, have been ignored, passed over, not listened to at times by significant people in your life. You can relate to this as well. Think of those experiences where nobody was there for you; when no one listened or cared about your thoughts and feelings; where no one stood in your world and saw it from your point of view. How alone you felt. How difficult it was for you to feel good about yourself, to pat yourself on the back and say, "Yes, I'm okay."

On the other hand, you have undoubtedly also had the experience of being noticed and attended to. Remember how it felt when your dad or mom took you out to breakfast alone, just the two of you? Remember when your parent picked you up and put you on his or her lap, sang songs to you, read books or just hugged you? Remember as an adult when you fell in love and that other person made you the center of his or her life? Those experiences dramatically told you that you existed. You existed because you were in relationship.

Your child needs to know that he or she exists. That's the basis for self-esteem. Amanda needs to feel that she's there and that she counts. Then she can go on to feeling good about herself. There is nothing more enriching and empowering than for children to know that what they say and do counts and makes a difference. All children born into this world need to know that they count. They know that when you and I pay attention to them.

Fortunately, the majority of children who come into this world receive attention at the beginning of their lives. They are born and fussed over. They can't help but feel noticed. Every whimper brings the parent running. But like anything else in life, children lose their novelty. Parents return to their own centers after a while, and children get ignored. Their pleadings for attention can become a nuisance instead of an opportunity to increase their self-esteem.

It's after that first wash of enthusiastic attention-giving that you, as a new parent, need to make the effort to keep on attending. Remember, your attention to your child tells her that she exists and that she counts. That's the starting point for positive self-esteem.

Every time you interact with your child, you demonstrate how valuable a creature your child is. Holding, talking to, playing with, stroking, caressing your child tells her that she matters and that she is valued.

As your child gets a little older, *listening* becomes the best way of attending to her. By respectfully listening, you tell your daughter that she is important and her thoughts and being are worthwhile. Certainly, when your child is little, she doesn't have a conscious awareness that you are attending to her, but she *experiences* it. That experience lets her know that she is of value. Attending to your child's world, her beliefs, feelings, values and behaviors tells her that she is okay just as she is. Even when your child says the worst thing possible to you— "Mommy, I hate you"—you still need to acknowledge the validity of your child's world. By recognizing and honoring your daughter's hostile feeling, you communicate to her a significant message: "Sandy, I know you're upset with me right now, and it's okay to be so. Having that strong feeling is neither good nor bad. It's just there. You are still a worthwhile, good girl, even though right now you're angry with me."

The best way of attending to your child, whether she

is one year old or 18 years old, is to listen to that child. When you listen, try not to jump too quickly to agreeing or disagreeing and to problem solving. One of the biggest mistakes you can make as a parent is to try too hard to help or save your child from hurt and harm. Saving and protecting your child comes later in the listening process. Most parents attempt to save and protect their children way too early.

To listen well, you must go through the following steps *in this order:*

1. Hear
2. Understand
3. Appreciate
4. Agree or disagree
5. Problem solve

As a parent you respond quickly to your children because that's what authority does. It jumps in to save the day and protect the innocent (or in the case of teenagers "the not-so-innocent"). Consequently, when you listen to your children you also attempt to react quickly. You jump from number 1, hearing, to number 4, disagreeing, or to number 5, problem solving. By skipping numbers 2 and 3, understanding and appreciating, you tell your children that what they are saying to you is not important. What is important is *your* opinion and *your* solution to the problem. Please resist the strong urge in you to react to the words your son is saying and to immediately disagree or tell him what to do or how to act.

Just listen well by understanding the ideas your son offers you and by appreciating what he feels. By doing so, you communicate to him that his ideas and his feelings are valuable and worthwhile. In a word, you are saying to him that *he* is worthwhile.

Self-esteem is improved more by your ability to listen respectfully to your son or daughter than by anything else you can do for your child. The more you work on this skill, the better your child will like him or herself.

Principle 4

**Compliment and criticize only your
child's behavior, not the child.**

"Of course," most parents think, "I'm not criticizing her. I'm just trying to correct her behavior." "I wouldn't call my daughter names," a mother protested in my office immediately after she commented to her daughter: "You're turning into a very unlovable girl, you know that?"

Listen closely to the talk you hear in the grocery store, the mall, at the zoo, in church, anywhere at all. Listen to the way parents talk to their children. You will be shocked at how frequently parents criticize their children, calling them names and putting them down.

Dad yanks Darlene by the arm and snaps: "Get over here right now. You're a bad girl."

Grandma tells Eric: "You have to study harder, or you'll grow up and become a good-for-nothing."

Grandpa changes Frankie's messy diaper (that will be the day!) and says: "Naughty boy, going doo-doo in your pants."

Listen carefully and you hear:

"Bad boy, hitting your sister again."

"You're so irresponsible."

"How dumb can you be?"

"You are the laziest kid on the block."

"Can't you ever get anything right?"

"When are you going to grow up?"

"You're a real pain in the neck, you know it?"

You may have heard some of these phrases coming out of your own mouth. Or you may have heard them from your parents when you were a child. They slip out so easily when you're stressed and frustrated with your child's behavior. You may be saying these kinds of things without even noticing. So please don't be too quick to say: "Well, at least I don't call my children names."

Perhaps the most subtle way parents name-call is by camouflaging it through a question. Notice that in the examples above, several statements are in the form of questions. "How dumb can you be" is not really a question at all. It's a camouflaged statement. This question seeks no answer. It's attempting to communicate something about your child's intelligence, and not something very complimentary.

Oftentimes parents send messages to their children through questions. I recall asking my son when he was eight years old how many times I needed to tell him to stay out of the road when playing. He looked right up at me and said, "About twelve times, Dad." I didn't want to hear that answer or any answer from him. So I said to him, "Don't be a smart aleck, young man." You see, I called him a name.

If you say to your son, "How dumb can you be?" you don't want an answer such as, "Well, Dad, on my standardized tests I scored in the 89th percentile on math and reading skills, and in the 92nd percentile on motor skills. Not bad, hey?" If he says that to you, you will be ready to tell him what you think of his quick mouth. Basically, you're trying to tell your son that he *is* dumb when you ask the question, "How dumb can you be?" This is a powerful form of name-calling because it's indirect. It slides into your child's subconscious mind without him even noticing. So watch your questions that convey indirect negative messages about your children. Such messages eat away at positive self-esteem.

Try to disconnect your child's behavior from his or her person. What Mary *does* fails to equal *who* Mary *is*. She is not a "bad girl" because she says "no" to her mother's request for help. In fact, Mary is a good girl who is simply saying "no" more often than you might like. John is not a "good boy" because he got all A's on his report card. He is a good boy, period. He happened to get all A's.

Stay focused on behavior, both positive and negative. If Timmy did a good job of brushing his teeth, say: "Timmy, you sure got all those teeth brushed tonight." You acknowledge what he did. You don't judge *him* to be a good person because he brushed his teeth well.

Compliment behaviors rather than the person. Say, for example:

"You did that homework very well tonight."

"You certainly worked hard on that project."

"Your room looks exceptionally clean today."

"I like how you talk to Grandma on the phone."

"Thanks for picking up your toys in the basement. I appreciate that."

"I'm glad you took the dog for a walk today."

"I'm sure your brother was delighted that you played that game with him."

You get the idea? Children are not good because they do these things. They are good children who sometimes (or oftentimes) do helpful things, and who, at other times, do things that you don't appreciate. But they are always good children.

When our children were very young, the girl next door, Terry, babysat for them. She was 11 when she started sitting. The first time we came home I asked Terry how the kids behaved. She said: "Andy and Amy were good kids tonight. They went to bed right away." Ah, I thought, a teachable moment. I said to Terry, "Andy and Amy are always good children, Terry. Sometimes their behavior might not be so great and other times it will be fine. But they are always good kids." This 11-year-old looked at me with a blank stare that said I had just communicated with a flower pot. So much for the "teachable moment."

Terry babysat for our children until she finished high school. She related to them wonderfully and they adored her. Throughout the years, on returning home from an evening out, I would ask her how the children behaved. She would say they were good or bad. I would always comment: "They are always good. It's just that sometimes they don't act in the best ways."

After seven years of babysitting, Terry surprised me one evening at the end of a rather gruelling session of sitting for the children. When I asked how the kids were, Terry responded: "Andy and Amy are very good children and they always are so. But their behavior tonight stunk." She got it. Even though I wasn't happy with her report about our children's behavior, Terry had separated *who* the children were from *what* they had done. Now, years later, I hope she still understands and believes this important distinction.

You might be thinking, "What difference does all this make anyway? My child doesn't make the distinction when I criticize her behavior and not her." You're probably right that she doesn't make the distinction intellectually: "Oh yes, my parents are criticizing my behavior, but clearly not me." This distinction actually has more immediate importance for *you* than for your children. If you are aware of viewing your children's behaviors as distinct from who they are, then you will *always* value the children no matter what they do or don't do. If you possess that spirit, your children will experience it from you. You communicate your valuing of them because your whole orientation is geared toward the children as good human beings independent of what they do.

If you believe that your children are good human beings no matter what they do or don't do, that message gets communicated to them. Children often misbehave to see if they are still loved by Dad and Mom. It's a way of testing their own self-esteem. When they experience our ongoing love and belief in their goodness, then they know that who they are is good, no matter what they do.

But is there ever a time to call your children positive names, to make statements about who they are? Yes, when they are doing *nothing*, or when you can disconnect your statement about the children from their behavior.

When Tammy is just sitting there, doing nothing, you can say to her: "Tammy, you know what? I think you're a really neat kid." Or "Tammy, I really love you." Or "Tammy, I sure value who you are."

Here you're making a statement about Tammy. It has nothing to do with how she is behaving or performing. Plain and simple, you're telling Tammy she is a good human being. That's a vital message in building positive self-esteem.

Young children usually accept such statements. And they often return similar statements to you. When you say to a youngster, "Kyle, I really like you," Kyle is likely to say to you, "I like you too, Mom." Older children, preteens and teens, may react more negatively, especially if they have not been used to hearing such words from you.

If you have not made these kinds of positive statements to your teenager before, and now you're going to start doing so, she will probably resist your positive expression. You say to Megan, "You know, you really are a neat kid, Megan," and she's likely to answer, "Aw, Mom, cut it out. That's so dumb." Don't feel bad if that happens. Megan simply doesn't know what to do with your expression of endearment. The best thing you can do is receive Megan's discomfort and let her know again that you think she's neat. You might say:

"Megan, I know that sounds sort of dumb to you, but I mean it. I think you're a neat kid."

"Mom," she protests, "don't say that anymore. I can't believe you're talking like that."

Then you say, "Okay, I'll watch my tongue. But it's still true." And you leave her alone.

A week later you might say something again to her. "Hey, Megan, I know you might think this is goofy for me to say, but I love you."

"Mom," she pleads.

But by that time you have fled the room. You have just dropped a little seed of love in the garden of Megan's self-concept. You've told her she's lovable just by being there. Nothing more, nothing less.

Even if Megan complains about your loving statements, she's still getting the message, and that's the important piece. The message you're imprinting deep within her heart is: "Independently of anything I do or don't do, my mom values me as a good person."

Focus, then, on complimenting and criticizing your children's behavior, never your children. When nothing special is happening, simply tell them how great they are and how much you love them. Once you start doing this with your young children, don't quit as they get older. Keep it up. More important than feeding their bodies with nutritious food, feed their hearts with the vitamins of your love and your constant view of them as good human beings who are capable of living full and satisfying lives.

Principle 5

Keep telling yourself that "kids are kids."

That sounds fairly straightforward and quite obvious, doesn't it? Sitting calmly, reading this book, you can agree with this basic principle. Children are children and they act that way all the time. But when you're in the heat of the action with your children, you easily forget this little principle and believe your children should think and act as adults would in the same situation. No. It doesn't work that way, and you need to continually remind yourself of that.

Your expectations of children shift dramatically between two and three years of age. Because they can talk by that time, you believe they can reason just as you can. When they were infants you allowed for irrational and random behavior from them: whining, spilling milk, spontaneous screaming, impulsive hitting, and chewing whatever fit in their mouths. These were tolerable activities, even though frustrating. But when they reached age two, your expectations changed. They could understand your words. So of course they should be able to understand your ideas. Now when you tell them once to stop whining or to keep their milk in the cup, you think they should be able to do just that. There's your mistake. Just because you say things to children, it doesn't at all mean they "got it." In fact, because they are "just kids," they probably *didn't* get it. So they keep right on doing the same "irresponsible" things they did when they were infants.

You know that you're expecting your children to act as adults and are rejecting the principle "kids are kids" if you hear yourself telling them to "grow up." This phrase reveals your real expectations; namely, that from age two on, your children should function as little adults.

Furthermore, telling your children to "grow up" is a name-calling statement. What you're really saying to them is: "You are very immature and shouldn't be as you are. You are not acceptable this way and I want you to change. In fact, I do not accept you as a child. I will accept you only as a young adult."

Another phrase that parents often use with their children is: "I can't believe you did that"—usually said with shock and dismay. This statement also betrays your belief that kids are not supposed to be kids. Of course what kids do is believable. They are kids and do things that you will think are irresponsible and nonsensical. That's part of what it means to be a kid. When you say "I can't believe you did that," you really mean "I was fully expecting more adult behavior and judgment from you."

Six-year-old Peter is discovered by his mother in the living room with his sand toys, Tonka truck and all. The rubber tree is out of its giant pot and Peter is excavating the plant holder. All the dirt is strewn across the new yellow carpet. It's a mess.

Most parents, understandably, would react in an upset manner. Peter "knew" he wasn't supposed to play in the living room. Any rational adult would know that you don't play "excavation-of-plants" on a new yellow, expensive carpet. And Peter, who is six, should know better, you think. He should *know* how to think as you would. *But Peter doesn't know how to think as an adult.* He is a child growing up. And kids growing up have significant lapses of rational thought. They regress at times to infant-like thinking and behaviors. That's why you might occasionally hear yourself saying something like: "You're acting like a two-year-old."

Young children don't have clear boundaries wrapped around their thinking or their behaviors. Part of their growing up means figuring out how to operate in the world around them. The way children learn to do that is by trying out things spontaneously and making mistakes. Gradually—and I do mean gradually—they learn. You can certainly encourage your children to learn how to think and act in appropriate ways, but you need to understand that the operative word here is "gradually." They learn to think and act as responsible adults little by little. By "gradually" I mean by the time they are 22! Really, don't expect perfect adult responses until they leave home. Even then, don't be surprised by their judgments and decisions. When you think about it, even we wise and experienced adults still do things and make judgments that can be described as "childish." At least once in a while!

So children fluctuate. That's what makes them so fascinating, challenging and frustrating. Just when you think they're growing up and able to be trusted in making some decisions, they regress and do something that startles you. The teenager who uses the car in a responsible manner calls you from the police station and says the police stopped her because she had a carload of kids who were drinking beer. Surprise. "That's just not like Allison," you say. "I don't understand her."

That may not be the way Allison normally functions, but it is how kids growing up behave at times. Children of all ages gradually behave in more rational ways, but all along the journey they have moments of regression. When they do regress, they behave with the judgments and reactions of much younger children. That surprises you and often triggers your frustration.

Kids are kids. They flip from acting at times as young adults and at other times as little children. The more you realize that fact, the more accepting of your children you will become. And accepting your children as "persons-on-a-journey-to-growing-up" will allow them to also accept themselves as good and capable human beings.

Principle 6

Focus on and encourage the *process* of your children's lives rather than the *content*.

The content of a child's life consists of the quantified outcomes of his or her activity. The results of content can be measured. Examples include:

1. The number of points she scored in the game.
2. The grades he got on his report card.
3. The amount of money earned from the paper route.
4. All the vegetables eaten off the plate.
5. The number of friends your child has.
6. Mastering the task of riding a two-wheeled bike.
7. Talking in full sentences.
8. Being able to add and subtract.
9. Your daughter getting her driver's license.

Content is the end product—made up of successes and failures, victories and defeats. *Process*, on the other hand, is the personal quality or style your child brings to the content. Process is the *way* your child does things, the friendly way she greets her friends, the intensity he brings to the soccer game, the persistent way she sticks to her studies, the light-heartedness he displays in the morning, the gentle manner she uses with the dog, and the sense of fairness he brings to all his games.

Process reflects characteristics about the child. The way your child does things reveals who your child is. In the context of your child's self-esteem, process stands head and shoulders above content.

Do you see the difference? The old adage might help: "It's not whether you win or lose, but how you play the game that counts." A child can get straight A's on her report card and brag to everyone about the level of her brilliance. Or she can accept the grades in a graceful way as an imperfect measure of her intellectual capacity and diligence. The process is much more significant than the content. You help your child's sense of worth by highlighting the processes of her life rather than by focusing on her successes and failures.

Every human being, and therefore every child, displays qualities of goodness and strength. One child shows considerable empathy toward other children; another demonstrates perseverance in performing a task; another displays an inquisitive mind. These qualities come from within the child and make up the "stuff" of the child. This is, in part, *who* the child is. Making the team or eating all his food does not make Freddy be Freddy.

However, as mentioned earlier, our society tends to equate who a person *is* with what he or she has accomplished. Society's belief is, "Freddy *is* his content. He *is* his accomplishments. He *is* his successes and his failures." Society believes that Freddy is a winner or a loser based on the end product of his behavior.

Your task as a parent is counter-cultural. In other words, you need to send Freddy a very different message from the one society preaches. You need to help Freddy realize that the way he does things—the way he relates, studies, plays and works—is what makes him a worthwhile person. Then, whether Freddy scores 20 points in the basketball game or sits on the bench cheering his team on becomes less important than his being a positive influence on his teammates.

Susy complains "I can't do anything right" when she drops her baton in the parade. That's a statement about content. She has not succeeded in her own mind. Based on that failing experience, she makes a statement about her person: "I can't do anything right." It's an easy next step for her to say: "Therefore, *I* am a failure." Because she focused on the content of her life she drew a negative conclusion about herself.

This is where Susy's parents can be helpful to her by attending more to the process of marching in the parade than to the content of it (dropping her baton six times). In this case, Susy's parents zero in on her exuberance while marching. She walked with a bounce in her step, a broad smile on her face. She winked at little kids sitting on the curb, and she even waved while twirling. People enjoyed her as she passed by. The occasional dropped baton made little difference to the parents and to the adults and children watching the parade. The quality of joy and delight Susy presented spoke much more powerfully about the kind of person she was.

To reinforce the focus on process rather than content, Susy's parents might say something like this to her: "Susy, I know you feel sad about dropping that baton." (Remember, first you want to *receive* your child's feeling no matter what it is.) Then, a little bit later, they might go back to her and comment: "You know, darling, something I really value about you is how much joy and life flows out of you. For example, this morning in the parade I could see how much joy you gave to people along the route by your smile and waving. That's really neat about you."

Do you get the idea? You acknowledge your child's feelings because she's focused on the content; but then highlight for her the wonderful process she uses and let her know that's what you value.

Here are some examples of processes you can identify and things you can say to reinforce your child's self-esteem:
- "That's so cute how you cuddle with the dog."
- "It's so impressive to me that you get right to your homework."
- "I appreciate your helping me when I know you'd rather be out playing."
- "I like how you talk to Grandma. I'm sure it means a lot to her that you talk with her."
- "I'm glad you're so nice to your little sister."

- "You have such a positive attitude toward everything."
- "Your smile warms my day." (That one might not work too well with a teenager!)

You can even identify your child's processes—and compliment them—when the behavior is negative. For example:

- "Even though you get so upset sometimes, I like the energy and passion you have for things."
- "I know you like to negotiate, and sometimes that gets annoying for me. But you certainly have a lot of perseverance. I respect that about you."
- "Being sensitive sometimes makes you have hurt feelings, but it also helps you tune into others' feelings, and that's neat."
- "I don't like it when you break the rules at home and school, but I do like your spirit of freedom."

You need to correct and control some of your child's behavior. But afterwards, when the emotion and energy have given way to peace and calm, you can let your child know that even in her mistakes there are aspects of her behavior that are positive. They just need some structure and direction at times.

When my daughter had her temporary driver's license, she took the car out one day by herself "just to see what it was like to drive alone." My wife and I didn't find out until some time later. My first reaction was upset.

"Amy," I complained, "that's the perfect way not to get your license. What if a police officer stopped you? You wouldn't get your license until you were eighteen."

Fortunately, she didn't get into an accident, didn't get hurt, didn't hurt anyone or anything else. Also fortunately, she didn't get stopped by the police. A couple of days later, when I had settled down, I said to my daughter: "Amy, I think it was a poor decision to take the car out alone because of what could have happened. But I must admit, I do admire your spunk and your sense of personal freedom." We then had an interesting conversation about teenagers taking risks, about "magical thinking," and about stopping to think things through before spontaneously jumping into potentially dangerous activities.

I have found it to be a helpful exercise at times to think about and identify those processes or qualities that my children possess that are life-giving and positive. When they were young, I stood at the foot of their beds while they slept reflecting on their positive qualities. Somehow, it seemed easier to identify such characteristics when they had their eyes closed. (Now, of course, I am asleep long before they are. Perhaps they sneak into my bedroom now and ponder my positive qualities. Don't I wish!)

By identifying those positive qualities in your children's lives, you focus on them. The more you focus on those aspects, the more you express them to your children. The more you identify and express them to your children, the more likely they will value those qualities and use them as an accurate basis for their own self-esteem. Your children are good people because they possess life-giving qualities, not because they have done well or poorly at some task.

Principle 7

Teach your children that their experience is valid even if it differs from the experience of others.

As I discussed in the first section of this book, most children develop a subtle and powerful belief—one embedded deeply in Western culture—that "If your world and mine differ, one of our worlds is invalid and must go." We believe that opposites cannot stand alongside each other. Something cannot be both right and wrong, fast and slow, black and white, hot and cold, all at the same time. If your child disagrees with you, then one of you must be right and the other wrong. One wins, the other loses.

We Westerners think that way. When a difference occurs, your child—much like you, no doubt—figures one view is correct and the other is incorrect. Of course, your child—much like you, no doubt—fights for the correctness of his view. When your child regularly invalidates his view, he feels inferior, hurt and overly sensitive. When he routinely invalidates other people's worlds, he feels angry, aggressive and superior to them. Both responses signal poor self-esteem.

From early on in your child's life, try to dislodge this insidious and irrational belief. In reality, two opposing views or experiences can both be valid. They can stand alongside each other. They are both valid, only different. When your son says his sister started the fight and you saw him hit her first, each of you has a valid view. They are just different. He believes she egged him on, taunting and teasing him. He believes that's what started the fight. You saw him hit her without apparent provocation. You believe that's what started the fight. Seen through your son's eyes, his view is understandable. You may disagree with it. That's fine. However, it is still understandable that he concluded she started the fight. Through understanding, you validate your son's view. You can then disagree with that view by stating your own view. Just as his view is valid, so is yours. The views are merely different.

I've always believed that validating and accepting another person's position when it differs from your own is a sure sign of high self-esteem. To respectfully listen to and appreciate another's view that is different from your own can be done only if you're not being defensive about your own view. And if you're secure enough with yourself, you don't need to defend your world view when someone else's differs. A different view does not mean an attack on your view. Furthermore, it doesn't mean your view is "wrong" or that you are stupid, dumb or a bad person. It merely means someone sees the world in a way you don't. This doesn't make him or her wrong or bad. Nor does it make you inept or ignorant.

You can see where this discussion is going. For you to help your child grow in self-esteem, you need positive self-esteem yourself. You need to feel secure with yourself and secure with your own points of view. You need to be well grounded, so that if your child disagrees with you, it doesn't make you defensive or insecure. Believing in yourself aids you in comfortably holding and honoring your own beliefs on any issue. Valuing yourself also allows you to temporarily let go of your views and positions in order to fully understand and honor your child's views.

Tolerance, understanding, appreciation, honor and respect are all words that come to mind when I try to describe the stance you want to take toward your child in building her self-esteem.

First, you need to apply these words to yourself, then to your child. The best way to gain this tolerant and respecting stance toward your child is to receive your child in a non-judging manner. Regarding my children, I tell myself often: "Dale, no one made you the judge." Certainly I have opinions on what would be helpful and useful for my children and what would be hurtful to them. And at some point I can tell them my opinion. But at no point can I judge them to be good or bad solely because they have opinions and views different from my own.

By listening respectfully to your child's views, momentarily letting your views fall to the background, you tell your child that both her world and she, as a person, are valid and okay. She and her view count.

To honor your child's views without dishonoring your own, you need to slow down. It's very easy to disrespect your child by quickly jumping in with your opinion and your judgment. Because you love your child, you want her to be safe. You aren't sure of her judgment, whether she's six or 16. So when she tells you she can walk alone to her friend's house, you jump right in and say, "No way. You're too young to cross the street yourself," or "No way. You can't be out on the street at ten o'clock at night."

By reacting quickly, you're attempting to protect your child from possible harm. That's perfectly valid and understandable. But if you pounce on your child's idea like a cat on a mouse, you invalidate her position and in the process you invalidate her.

Slow down. Slow down. Slow down.

Give your child's self-esteem a big boost. Take a deep breath and listen. Remember the steps in listening well that I describe on page 48. Because this process of listening is so important, I want to tell it to you again:

1. Hear what she says.
2. Understand what she means.
3. Appreciate her feelings and point of view.
4. Agree or disagree with her only after taking steps 1 through 3.
5. And finally, help solve her problem if there is one.

See how slowly you need to go in order to listen well? Unfortunately, most of us parents don't listen well to our children. We tend to hear the words our children speak and jump to disagree, advise or problem solve right away. We're not so good at understanding and appreciating. And those are the two steps that validate our children's experience and affirm their positive sense of self.

Here's an exercise for you to practice in communicating with your children. It will help you slow down, and it will strengthen your children's self-esteem. For one week, try as hard as you can to listen to your children by using only steps 1, 2 and 3 in the listening process described above. Hear your children, make sure you understand what they are saying, and, most difficult of all, appreciate their points of view—even if you disagree with them. Hear, understand and appreciate. Try your hardest not to jump from hearing your children (step 1) to disagreeing with them (step 4) or to solving their problems (step 5) before you have understood them (step 2) and appreciated their experience (step 3).

This will be hard to do. And I realize that at times you will have to disagree or problem-solve with them. But before you do so, first understand and appreciate. Let them know that you received their message and that you value their point of view. Only after spending some time *understanding* and *appreciating* can you then disagree.

After you have done this for a week, I'm sure you'll want to do it for another week, and another. By understanding and appreciating your children's worlds you teach them that their positions are valid *and* so are yours. *Both* worlds can exist side by side even if they are different. One person or view need not be right and the other wrong. One is not good and the other bad. One doesn't need to come away the winner and the other the loser. What a wonderful message to send to your children: You and your experience are valid and demand respect. You are not good or bad because you are different. You are unique, that's all.

Principle 8

Teach your children to be optimistic rather than pessimistic.

If you're a doom-and-gloom thinker, chances are your child will become one also. Do you see the half-full glass or the half-empty glass? Children with low self-esteem anticipate the worst; thus, the worst likely happens. They're convinced they can't ever learn to ride a two-wheel bike. They get a poor grade on a paper and say: "I'm so dumb." They get to the free throw line at a critical moment in a game and think: "I know I'm going to miss this shot." They fully believe no one will ask them to the homecoming dance. They think they're ugly. They feel uncoordinated.

These children plan for the worst, they predict it, and then they go out and fulfill their predictions. As a result their failures reinforce their negative self-concept. They have just proven to themselves, and to anyone willing to watch, how awful they really are.

At least three factors go into the development of a pessimistic attitude. Social psychologist Martin Seligman, in his book *Learned Optimism* (Knopf, 1990), tells us what they are:

1. Mom's way of thinking.
2. Adult criticism.

3. Children's early life crises and losses.

Perhaps none of the three factors is as important and powerful as the influence of the mother's pessimism or optimism on her children. In studies reported in *Learned Optimism*, the children's optimistic or pessimistic attitudes were closely related to those of the mother. This was true for boys and girls. Interestingly, the father's optimism or pessimism didn't influence the children's attitudes much at all. Because moms are the primary caretakers in most families, it's *their* thinking style that shapes the attitudes of their children.

One mother continually worried about her daughter's overeating. When the mother had been young herself, she had felt heavy and ugly. She had felt terrible about herself. She didn't want her daughter to go through that, so Mom stayed ever vigilant, steering Ann away from fat foods and frequently warning her that eating the wrong foods would lead to her getting fat. Pessimistically, Mom was already believing her daughter would become fat like she did as a child. As Mom worried, preaching the vices of sugar and fats and watching closely over Ann, she was creating an attitude about weight, body image and food for Ann to incorporate.

The picture created in Ann's mind was that of a fat girl, because that's the image Mom kept sending her, even though she was saying "not" to be fat. When telling a child "not," you first paint a picture of what you're talking about. In other words, to tell a child, "Don't eat so much candy on Halloween," the child has to first have a picture in her mind that sees herself eating a lot of candy. The word "not" draws a red line through the picture, but the picture is still there.

Children become the images they have of themselves. Mom kept sending Ann an image of herself as overweight and unattractive, even though she was trying to help her daughter avoid such a result. Mom's fear and continual focus on being overweight created an image in her daughter. Ann then lived out the image and became overweight.

There's an old saying that applies to parents: "Our children are the products of our hopes or fears." If you live fearing what might happen to your children, it's more likely that what you fear will come to pass. If you hope for your children, it's more likely that they will live out your hopes.

When my daughter, Amy, was four years old, she wanted to help me make breakfast one Sunday morning. She asked if she could get the eggs from the refrigerator. I said, "Yes, but don't drop them." You see the problem.

For Amy to make sense of what I just said, she had to create a picture in her mind of taking the eggs out of the refrigerator and promptly dropping them on the floor. Her logical brain then came along and said "Now, don't do that." But the image was already planted. And she lived it out. She picked up the tray of eggs and they "accidentally" slipped out of her hands.

We call this a "self-fulfilling prophecy." I was thinking pessimistically about her ability to help me. I presented that pessimistic picture to her. She put it up on her mental computer screen and performed accordingly.

What I learned from this experience was to try to present positive images to my children, not negative images. I should have said to Amy: "Yes, you can help. Open the refrigerator door and gently lift out one egg in one hand and one egg in the other hand." You see the difference. Here I'm painting a positive picture for her of exactly how a successful interaction with eggs can work.

After our egg encounter I realized how often I spoke negatively to my children. Here are some examples:

- "Get away from those steps before you fall down them."
- "You'll choke on that food if you eat so fast." (Fortunately this one never came to pass.)
- "Don't write with chalk on the bricks."
- "Now, be sure you don't fight with each other while we're gone."
- "Try not to spend all your money on bubble gum."
- "Don't exceed the speed limit when you drive."

Instead of this negative approach, presenting more positive images could have led to more positive behavior. I could have said:

- "I'd like you to play over here in the center of the room."
- "Use the chalk only on the driveway."

- "Take your time eating. Chew your food slowly. Put your fork down between bites."
- "While we're gone tonight, I want you two to cooperate and enjoy one another."
- "Why don't you spend this one dollar on gum and put the rest in your bank?"
- "Be sure you drive 55 mph on the freeway."

Here I'm being positive, describing exactly the behavior I want from my children. Children tend to live out the images you create for them, so it's vital that you create positive, constructive images.

That needs to extend beyond their behavior to the children themselves. Do all you can to create positive pictures of your children. Certainly, at times you must criticize their behavior. But as I explained in Principle 3, never call them names or infer images of them as dumb, inadequate, incapable, bad or villainous. Instead, keep sending positive images, saying things like, "I know you're a caring kid, even when you get mad." "I believe in you, so I know you can do that if you want to." "I can see you doing well in that test tomorrow." "I have always sensed that you are a creative child."

In this way, your child lives out your hopes and positive images rather than your fears and negative pictures.

The second factor leading to pessimistic thinking is *adult criticism.* The more that parents, teachers, pastors and coaches criticize children, the more likely the children develop pessimistic attitudes and low self-esteem. In hoping that your children grow up to live satisfying and successful lives, it's fairly easy to push them and shape them according to your own expectations. When they don't measure up, then it's time for criticism.

A disturbing result has appeared in the research about how boys and girls are criticized. In school situations, when boys fail, teachers' criticisms tend to be specific. Teachers say: "You didn't try hard enough this time." "You weren't paying attention when I taught this in class." "You confused this week's material with last week's." Teachers attribute the failure of boys to a particular cause rather than to a universal or character cause.

Teachers' criticism of girls, on the other hand, tends to zero in on pervasive personality characteristics that cannot be changed. When girls fail, teachers criticize by saying: "You don't have a mathematical mind." "You're always disorganized in your work." "Your mind is always somewhere else."

These criticisms are directed at the girls themselves. They are statements about things they cannot change, whereas with boys, the criticisms are aimed at some external circumstance that can be changed. So girls learn they don't have any power to become different. That makes them feel helpless and hopeless, a most pessimistic mindset. If they can't change, can't get the math or science, then they must be dumb. Being dumb, of course, opens the door to low self-esteem.

Being critical of your children, then, is something that needs close monitoring. If you are critical, be sure it is done optimistically. By that I mean giving your child a way out. Make your criticisms *temporary, specific and non-personal.*

Temporary:
- "This time, you did a poor job washing the dishes."
- "This quarter, your grades slipped because you didn't spend enough time on homework."
- "Sometimes you talk mean to me."

Specific:
- "This school assignment is pretty messy."
- "Your sand toys are outside your box."
- "Hold your fork the proper way when you eat."

Non-personal:
- "You didn't take the garbage out. I need that done."
- "Please clean out all the food stuff in your room. It's starting to smell in there."
- "Your music is really hard on my ears."

Pessimistic criticisms, according to Seligman, are *permanent, pervasive and personal.* Using the same examples, they would sound like this:

Permanent:
- "You just can't get that dishwashing thing right, can you?"
- "No wonder your grades stink. You *never* spend enough time on homework."
- "You always mouth off to me."

Pervasive:

- "You're so disorganized when it comes to school work."
- "Your toys are forever strewn all over creation."
- "You have absolutely no manners whatsoever."

Personal:

- "You're so irresponsible. I give you one simple task and you can't even do it."
- "That's not music you're listening to. That's noise. You'll never know what good music is."
- "Your room is a pig sty and you're the pig who lives in it."

When criticisms are permanent, pervasive and personal, they create a sense of helplessness in the child. These criticisms tell the child that he is deformed, disabled and disgusting. And he can't change even if he wanted to. So watch how you criticize. The less you do the better. But if you have to criticize, and you will, then make it "optimistic criticism." Stay focused on the present behavior you want changed. And give your child hope that he or she can make that change. Keep believing in the goodness of your child.

The third factor influencing children's pessimistic thinking involves the early life crises they have experienced. The more difficult a child's life experiences, the more likely he or she will think pessimistically. The death of the mother before the child reaches teenage years plays a significant role in the development of a child's pessimistic style of thinking. Divorce also leads toward pessimistic thinking and depression in children, even several years after the divorce.

Short of divorce, fighting in a family system tends to increase a child's pessimistic thinking and leads to depression. Depression usually involves low self-esteem. Here's where you have a chance to help your child. Don't fight! Particularly, don't fight with your spouse. Think about it when a fight is brewing. Do you want to get hooked into the fight? Are there any other ways of dealing with the conflict where you can remain empowered?

By saying "Don't fight" I'm not suggesting you allow your partner to verbally or physically abuse you. On the contrary, look for creative ways to disengage from the fight while maintaining and honoring your own position. The point I want to make is that children raised in a fighting environment tend to grow up thinking more pessimistically than those raised in a more peaceful family.

While you cannot control all the negative experiences a child encounters in early life, you probably can reduce the impact of them by staying close to your child, by displaying an optimistic attitude and by creating a calm and harmonious environment. At least within the home, your ability to build peaceful relationships will go a long way toward helping your child think in optimistic and, consequently, positive ways about him or herself.

Principle 9

Use a technique of identifying with a hero.

Children with low self-esteem think negatively; those with high self-esteem think positively. Your job? Help your child create positive thoughts about him or herself. One way of doing this is to get your child to identify someone he admires. Then help your child figure out how that person thinks, what kind of attitudes that person carries into life and how that person behaves.

You can do this with children of any age over four or five.

Let's take eight-year-old Danny. This young boy likes sports, but doesn't think he's any good in the games the kids play. He gets picked late in the selection process. He rarely has the chance to be captain. He's afraid he will make a mistake and get yelled at by the other kids.

You sit down with Danny and ask: "Danny, is there any player in the whole world in any sport that you really like and think is outstanding?"

Danny can tell you that right away. He says, "Yeah, Michael Jordan."

So you begin raising questions about Michael Jordan: "What do you think Michael Jordan does before a game?"

"Well, he probably eats a steak dinner in the afternoon. Then watches some TV. That's about it."

Danny's now thinking about his hero and what Jordan does, rather than about how badly he, Danny, plays basketball.

You say, "Then what?" Your job is to keep Danny focused on his hero, on what he does, how he thinks, what attitudes he carries.

"Well, then he gets into his sports car and drives to the arena."

"While he's driving, what would you say he's thinking about?"

"He's probably planning how he's going to play against the other team."

"Like how?"

"Well, like thinking he can take the guy guarding him, fake him out and dribble closer to the basket and shoot."

"So, he sees himself doing those things, is that right?"

"Yeah, he sees himself faking out the guy guarding him and going in."

"When he sees himself shooting, does he make the shot?"

"Oh yeah. He never misses."

"Do you think he's nervous while driving to the game?"

"Sure, he's nervous."

"Like nervous-scared or nervous-excited?"

"Michael Jordan wouldn't be nervous-scared. He's not scared of anything. He'd be excited."

"Why would he be excited as he drives to the game?"

"Because he knows he's going to score 25 points, the fans will be screaming for him and his team will win."

"So he's excited because he knows he will do well, right?"

"Right."

"Or because he *believes* he will do well."

"I suppose."

"What if Michael Jordan were driving to the game thinking he wasn't going to score many points and was going to play a bad game. What do you think would happen then?"

"That wouldn't happen. He wouldn't think like that."

"But what if he did think like that?"

"Then he wouldn't be Michael Jordan. He'd be a loser."

"You know, I'll bet that Michael Jordan got so good because when he was a kid, he used to *think* that he was going to make the basket, win the game and get the trophy. Because he thought like that, it helped him get that way. He became good. Then the better he became, the easier it was to think good thoughts about himself. And the more he thought good thoughts, the better he played.

"I'm not saying you can be as good as Michael Jordan. But I bet if you thought just like he thought when he was going to a game, it might help you feel better and do better."

"But I'm no good at basketball...."

"But, you see, that's exactly what I mean. Because you believe you're no good, that's likely what will happen. Try picturing yourself playing in the game, driving to the basket, putting up the shot and scoring. See what that feels like."

Then ask Danny to close his eyes and picture himself playing a game successfully and scoring a basket.

End the conversation by saying, "Danny, the way you think, the picture you have of yourself in your mind, is the way you will actually play the game. That's how Jordan does it. That's how every successful athlete does it. And that's how you can do it too."

Then let the conversation go. Don't preach a lot. Just get Danny to think and imagine himself like his hero would think and imagine.

With teenagers, you don't need to ask them about a specific hero figure, unless they obviously have one. With teens you can ask a little more directly: "Kelly, what would you like to be like?"

She responds, "I want to be popular at school."

"What would you have to do to become popular?"

Teenagers often respond to this type of question with, "I don't know."

"Well," you persevere, "what do the kids who are popular do?"

"They kiss up a lot to teachers and other kids."

"What do you mean they kiss up?"

"Well, they act real nice in front of them, like they're interested in them."

"For them to show interest in the teachers or other kids, what do you think they think like? What's going on in their minds?"

"I don't know." (The famous teenage phrase!)

"Well, think about it some. If someone were trying to show interest in another person, what would she have to be thinking?"

"I don't know, maybe that the other person is worth listening to, that maybe she will feel better because I listened to her."

"So to show interest in another person you'd have to think she was worth listening to and it might make her feel better. Or another way of saying it might be, you'd be thinking mainly of her, not of yourself at the time."

"I guess so."

"I think those are good ideas, Kelly. And I think you're right. The way to become popular or liked by others is to pay attention to them, to believe they are worth listening to—and by listening you help them feel better. The result of that kind of thinking is that other people will probably feel better about you."

Again, make your point briefly and let it go. Don't lecture. In this process, you're getting your child to focus on the way he or she thinks.

Thinking negatively creates low self-esteem. Thinking positively generates high self-esteem. Simply telling your child to think differently won't help. Guiding him or her to think differently by identifying with a hero figure and sensing how that person must think gives you better access to the mind and heart of your child.

Don't expect this approach to work the first time. Be patient and consistent. Thoughts and attitudes about self don't change easily. You help your child challenge the thoughts that feed low self-esteem by indirectly and regularly helping him or her think like a winner, like a confident, self-assured person thinks. Positive thoughts create positive self-esteem.

Principle 10

Challenge your child's belief about the importance of what others think of him or her.

Many adults suffer from this problem as well as children. In our society, worth and value seem inseparably linked to what others think of us. If others like us, we must be okay. If they don't like us, we must not be okay. We come to believe that others' judgment of us determines our level of self-esteem.

Children think this way naturally. Karl Jung said that in the first half of life young people focus on the external world, paying attention to how people act and react to them, noticing how to fit in, figuring out how to navigate through life. All the antennae are directed outward.

So it's easy to understand that children grow up paying close attention to how Dad and Mom, teachers, coaches and friends react to them. Early on they figure out: "If I am liked by them, then I must be likeable. If I am not liked, I must be unlikeable."

While there is obviously some truth to that belief, it is not absolutely true. Certainly, children need to be liked and loved early on. But they don't need to be liked and loved by everyone all the time. Unfortunately, many kids grow up believing they must be loved and liked by absolutely everyone. That principle leads directly to low self-esteem. The healthier principle is: I need to be loved by *some* people consistently and steadily. But I do not need to be loved or liked by everyone all the time.

Therefore, your primary job is to serve as the stable loving influence in your child's life. If your love is unconditional and constant, then your child has an opportunity to break free from the notion that he or she is okay only if everyone is judging him or her positively.

First of all, make sure your love is constant and not dependent on your child's successes and failures. If you are accepting of your child only when he or she behaves in approved ways, then you are teaching and reinforcing this awful belief that he or she is okay only if others approve. No, you need to approve of this child no matter what behavior he or she serves up. As I discussed earlier in Principle 3, you always need to affirm the child. You can criticize or praise behavior, but you always support and love the child.

Your kids will test you on this, especially as they get older. It's almost as though they want to see if you'll love them no matter how hard they try to be unlikeable. Teenagers might dress in disgusting clothes, cut their hair and shave their heads in ways that exceed your most creative imagination. They might burp at the table, pass gas in the car and pick their teeth in the family room. They might swear, call you by your first name and utter monosyllabic responses to your requests for information.

These kids make themselves unappealing to you. "Do you still love me?" is the question they are asking. "Even if I look dopey, act crudely and talk dirty, will you still love me?"

Your answer needs to be a definite "yes."

As you read this, saying "yes" might seem pretty easy. Of course, you love your child no matter what he or she looks like or does. But at that future moment when he or she will be acting like someone directly out of a horror movie, you might have more difficulty demonstrating your abiding love for your child.

At those moments, or as quickly as possible after those moments, you need to back away from your anger, upset or criticism and realize that Patrick is checking out the world, trying to figure out how to be. He will learn to navigate in the world well if you give him the stability of your love no matter how he behaves or looks.

By saying that, I do not mean to suggest that you fold your arms, stand back and let him do anything he wants. No. You can and need to have your rules and set the norms for him to follow. But when he does things that don't hurt himself or others or put him into positions where there is potential for harm, then you need to accept him and let go of your demand that he act like you.

One father nearly kicked his teenaged son out of the house when the boy appeared at the supper table one evening with a gold stud pierced through his ear. The father called the boy a wimp (among other things), grounded him and took away his allowance. He told the boy that he disgusted him, and he didn't want to see him again until that earring was gone. So what did this boy learn? That I am not likeable if I do something my father disagrees with.

In this instance a much better approach was reported to me by a set of parents. Their 15-year-old son asked if he could talk to them about an important issue. He then asked permission to get his ear pierced. He wanted to wear an earring. He had asked when he was 13 and his parents said no, not until he was 16. So here he was now a year early in his request. He explained why he wanted the earring, but before he got into his major selling points, his parents said it would be okay for him to do so.

The parents realized that their son was doing something that hurt no one, was a little deviant from the "norm," but was their son's way of being different and experimenting with how that felt. They were able to step back, accept their child as he tried on a new aspect of living, and show him he was just as acceptable and lovable whether he wore an earring or not.

I've always thought kids spend their lives observing their parents, taking mental notes on what parents like and don't like, what they value, and what they believe in deeply. By the time they are in their late preteen and teen years, they have a list of what's important to their parents. Then they start at the top of the list and do the opposite. If they know their parents value religious worship, the kids resist going to church. If the parents eat only nutritious food, then the kids chow down junk food. If the parents hate smoking, the kids leave cigarette packages strategically placed to be discovered. Children do things against the will and desire of parents, both to separate from the parents and to test their parents' abiding love.

Please try hard to pass this test your kids are giving you! It helps your children break free from the notions that only their perfect behavior makes them acceptable and that they're okay only if others judge them positively.

By loving them with an abiding love, you say to them: "You are not your behavior. Nor are you the judgments or opinions of other people. You are you, with your own behaviors and your own ways of doing things. And I accept and love you beyond your behaviors."

Again, I want to emphasize that by accepting and loving your children no matter what they do, you are not condoning their actions. You can clearly disagree with their behavior and with their attitudes. But these are not their defining characteristics. Your children are much more than their actions, thoughts or words.

Principle 11

Help your child find the inner source of his or her goodness.

Let me express it again. Your child is much more than her actions, thoughts or words. The way I have said it to people for years is this:

"You are not your behaviors. You are not your thoughts. You are not your feelings. You are certainly not the opinions of other people. You are none of those things. You are the energies of your heart. That's *who* you are."

I wish children the world over could learn this important truth. So many children and adults live only in the world of their behaviors and other people's reactions to their behaviors. They form their identities based on how they perform and whether the world applauds or not.

If I could wave a magic wand and change one aspect of human life, I would alter the focus of people's attention. I would direct them inward to their own heart and away from the forces outside of themselves that attempt to control who they are. The heart is the starting point for positive self-esteem. The heart contains powerful, rich energies that offer the basis of self-love and appreciation.

As a therapist for nearly three decades, I have seen people discover the goodness of their own hearts. Once they can separate their behaviors, thoughts and feelings from who they really are, they come alive in the appreciation of the energies of their hearts.

For children this is not an easy split to make. You can't say to a child: "Darling, you are not your behaviors, but the energies of your heart." You'd get back a blank stare from your child. But even though children can't make the split between the external world and the inner world of their own hearts, *you* can make that split and begin leading your children toward it as well. What do you have to do to help your children learn that they are the energies of their hearts rather than their behaviors or the opinions of others?

Step 1: Identify the energies of your child's heart.

We know what those energies are. In the journey to my own heart, and in walking with many others in the journey to their hearts, we keep arriving at the same places. I've been able to identify four energies that consistently arise from the depths of our hearts. They are the energies:

1. To exist.
2. To exist as fully as possible.
3. To be free.
4. To love and be loved.

"To exist" is evident. But I speak here not only of physical existence, but psychological and emotional existence as well. Your child wants desperately to exist. She cries for it, pouts for it, misbehaves-when-you're-on-the-telephone for it, draws you a picture for it, argues with you for it. When you notice, then she feels as if she exists. So your job is to notice, pay attention, and help her celebrate her existence.

"To exist as fully as possible" is the second energy of your child's heart. This energy propels your child toward happiness and fulfillment. It seeks contentment, delight, joy, satisfaction and well-being. Your child seeks those objects and performs those activities that she thinks will help her reach happiness and personal fulfillment. Sometimes she will be right and sometimes she will be wrong.

She chooses to study for the test, and when she takes it she gets an A. That choice leads to happiness. On Halloween, she decides to eat all the candy in her bag, thinking that will make her happy. She ends up sick and doesn't find pleasure. In either case, the energy for her behavior came from her heart. It was the energy "to exist as fully as possible."

Is that energy good? Absolutely. Was the behavior that arose from that energy helpful to her in getting the happy results she sought? In the case of studying, yes. In the case of Halloween candy, no. Is she a good girl because she studied for the test and got an A? No. Is she a bad girl because she ate the candy and got sick? No. Her behavior is secondary to the energy of her heart.

She is a good girl, acting out of a very good energy in her heart, the energy to exist fully. Unfortunately, the behavior that comes up from that energy sometimes gets detoured in a way, so that by the time it reaches the outside world, it doesn't really help her gain what she needs. But the behavior can be changed. That's what you do as a parent—help your daughter change and learn new behaviors that match better with the energies of her heart.

The third energy is to be "free." This powerful drive surges in your daughter. You've probably noticed it! It started to show that first time she said "no." She wants to put her toys in the box *her* way. She wants to stay up as late as her brother. She wants to eat cereal from the box. She wants to study at her own time of the day. She wants no curfew on the weekend.

Although some of these "freedom behaviors" your child serves up may annoy you or conflict with your values, they arise from an energy in her that is good—the energy to be free. She wants to be her own person, in charge of her own life (even though that's unrealistic at too early an age). The energy is good, the behaviors that bubble up from that energy sometimes work well and sometimes don't. But your daughter is not those behaviors. She is the energy of her heart. She is a free child, seeking to take hold of her own life. Great!

"To love and to be loved" is the final and perhaps the most evident energy. You see and feel your child snuggling with you, letting you stroke and kiss and hug her. You see her petting the dog and playing with her doll, mothering and loving it. You see her trying to connect to you by negotiating, complaining, fighting, yelling. Again, sometimes her behaviors bring about loving connections and other times they do the opposite. But either way, most of those behaviors are rising up from a loving heart. Your daughter *is* a loving child. Sometimes she acts that way and other times she doesn't. Okay, you work to help her change her behavior to better match her loving heart. But she still has a loving heart.

There you have the energies of the heart:

To exist.

To exist as fully as possible.

To be free.

To love and be loved.

Let those burn into your mind. And then look for them underneath your child's behavior.

Step 2: Focus on the energies of your child's heart rather than on her behaviors.

You give power to what you focus on. I've probably said those eight words more than any other set of words in my 20-plus years as a psychologist. What you pay attention to is what drives your life. What you notice and hold in your consciousness fuels your attitudes and emotions.

If all you can think about is the one negative comment your boss put on the evaluation, you give tremendous power to that comment and feel miserable the rest of the day, week or year. On the other hand, if you pay attention to her positive statement about your ability to close a deal, you are able to celebrate your skill.

Regarding self-esteem and your child, this principle needs to be applied to your child's behaviors and to his heart. As I indicated earlier, your child tends to focus on his behavior as the determinant of his self-esteem. Your job is to help him shift that focus and learn to attend to his heart. To do that, of course, you have to be able to notice his heart underneath his behaviors.

Often this is easy to do, especially when his behaviors match up with and reveal his heart directly. For instance, when he gently caresses his baby brother after the toddler falls down and is crying, you quickly identify that he *is* a loving child.

The same holds true when he tries hard at a game. Then you know he *is* a child who strives to be his best self. Or when he wants to try riding his two-wheeled bike without training wheels and alone, then you know he is a *free* child.

But there are times when you'll have to look hard underneath his behavior to find the positive energies of his heart. When he pushes his baby brother out of the way and knocks him down, then you'll have to go in search of the energy of freedom that cries out for space and independence from this little annoying creature.

You have to struggle to find his loving, connecting energy when he won't leave you alone while you're working. You have to get under his stubborn insistence on staying up later to discover the energy in him to live his life to the fullest.

You need to pay attention to the energies of your child's heart more than to his behaviors. That's hard because what you see directly are the behaviors, especially the annoying behaviors. You need to make a conscious, determined effort to slow down your reactions, think a little, and notice the energies under the behavior. If you have a young child, start this right away. Look for and identify the positive energies beneath your child's behavior. If you wait to do this when your son is 16, you'll have a lot of difficulty focusing on energies because his behavior will so dominate the scene.

By focusing on your child's energies instead of on his behavior, *you* begin to see your child as the "good boy" he is. His goodness is based on his heart, though, and not on his behaviors. Your ability to focus on his heart will, in itself, begin to transfer to him without you having to say anything at all. What you focus on will gradually become what he focuses on. Children pick up the values of the parents. What the parents value is what they focus on. So by attending to your son's heart energies, you are telling him, in effect, that you value *who* he is more so than what he does.

A word of caution: Please don't interpret what I'm saying here to mean that you should ignore your child's behavior entirely. At times people have objected to this point of view, saying that they can't just close their eyes to their child's behavior and focus on his heart's energies. Inappropriate behavior needs to be attended to, they say, and disciplined. I agree. By no means am I saying ignore your child's behavior, especially his negative behavior. No. Discipline is absolutely necessary. And, of course, to discipline, you need to pay attention to the behavior. That's fine.

But along with your attention to behavior, stop and think more deeply. See the energy underneath the behavior. Seeing it and affirming it will help you pass along the sense that your son is much more than just his behavior. And remember Principle 3: always separate—at least in your own mind—your son's behavior from who he is at his heart. He is always a good child, although his behavior at times may not be helpful or productive for him or others.

Step 3: Magnify the voice of your child's heart.

The energies at the core of your child speak to her with a thin and quiet voice. It's a whisper compared to the noisy boomboxes of the world around her. To hear the voice of her heart, she needs the boomboxes turned down and the volume of her heart turned up. It's pretty hard to silence the voices outside of her, the voices of the world telling her that she's only as good as her latest success.

But you can help her turn up the voice of her heart. Your job as her parent is to magnify the whispering voice of her heart so that she can hear who she is from inside of her rather than from outside of her.

Once *you* are able to identify the energies of your daughter's heart, you can then begin speaking of them to her. Your language needs to change a bit. At first, it might sound strange or unnatural. But stick with it. Eventually, it feels right.

When your four-year-old daughter rocks her baby sister to sleep, you say: "That was very good rocking. You put your sister to sleep pretty fast. You know, Jennifer, you are a very loving person." You see, first you praise Jennifer's behavior, then you make a separate comment about Jennifer's heart. You magnify the energy of love in her.

Later in the day, you're on the telephone and Jennifer begins pulling out pots and pans, making a racket, disturbing your phone call and waking up the baby. You get off the phone and say: "Jennifer, it's very hard for me to talk on the phone when you make so much noise. I don't want you to take the pots and pans out when I'm on the phone, do you understand?" After a little pause, then you say: "Jennifer, I know you're a very loving child and like to be with me. I like that too. When I'm on the phone, then I have to be connected to someone else. But in my heart I'm still connected to you."

Now Jennifer might not understand all of that. But say it anyway. She gets what she gets. Each time you say things like this, you're sending her important messages about her heart. Jennifer is always a good girl in her heart, even though pots-and-pans behaviors occur, sometimes all too frequently.

Here are other ways of magnifying your child's heart:

- "I don't like your temper tantrums, but I sure recognize a real passion in you to go for what you want."
- "You certainly study hard. Under that hard work I see a girl who wants to be her best self. That's neat!"
- "Although you don't always come home on time and that bothers me, I do recognize in you a real desire to be free and independent. That I want to encourage, although I'd still like you home on time."
- "I wish you wouldn't criticize your brother. I think that hurts his feelings. But I believe that under that criticism you really have a caring heart and just want what's best for him."

You see what I'm doing? Sometimes it's going to feel like a stretch for you. Politicians do this all the time. They put positive spins on everything they do. Parenting is not a political event. But when it comes to your child, you're trying to lead her to her heart. Acknowledge her behavior. Criticize or compliment it. But then, always try to make a positive statement about your child's heart.

Magnify that tiny voice inside your child. Uncover her beauty and power by first seeing the wonderful energies of her heart and then by telling her over and over again what you see beneath the behaviors she offers. *Your child is always a loving, free child, striving to be his or her very best self.* That's something to be celebrated, no matter how he or she behaves.

Principle 12

Send self-esteem messages to your children *indirectly* as well as directly.

Telling a child he's great is a marvelous thing to do. Telling him you love him is wonderful. Keep on doing that. But perhaps a more powerful way of helping him increase his self-esteem is to get the message to him *indirectly.* Indirect messages reach the child in a different way from direct messages, and they work at a deeper level.

Children under the age of 15 learn better through their bodies than through their minds. Their ability to abstract and conceptualize does not fully develop until mid-teen years. So early in life they learn through experience and through their *right brains.*

The right brain of your child is his visual, nonlinear brain. It forms a fairly direct path to the subconscious mind. The information it takes in travels deep within the child's psyche and gradually forms the attitudes and values the child comes to own.

The left brain, on the other hand, is more logical and linear in its process. It's the word brain, taking in messages and formulating those messages into thoughts and ideas. Often these ideas remain only in the head. They don't penetrate the psyche like the messages to the right brain do. That's why lecturing young children doesn't work very effectively. Even though the children hear the words, they remain "just words."

In helping your child develop attitudes, then, approaching him through his right brain becomes the "treatment of choice." To teach him positive attitudes about himself, your job is to send him messages *indirectly*.

Actually, when I think about all the aspects of parenting, I believe the most important is *sending positive messages to your child.* You give your child a most elegant gift when you consistently let him know what a good person he is. If parents the world over sent three positive messages to their children every day, I can't help but think our world would be a more peaceful and loving place.

Your job as a parent, then, is to send positive messages to your children. But send them *indirectly* more frequently than directly. How do you do that? I'm glad you asked. Here are six ways to teach positive self-esteem through the right brain:

1. Model high self-esteem yourself.
2. Quote the positive that others say about your child.
3. Tell your child stories.
4. Make reflective comments about events and people.
5. Talk to a third person so you're overheard by your child.

6. Tell your child positive things before and during sleep.

Let me explain each of these indirect strategies for improving self-esteem.

1. Model high self-esteem yourself.

Your child watches you closely. She imitates you. She parrots your words. She incorporates your attitudes, including your attitude about yourself. All this happens at a subconscious level. She's not sitting there taking notes on your behavior or your feelings. She's just absorbing whatever goes on around her. The way you are, the way you think, feel and behave—these travel on a highway through her right brain directly to her heart. If you're down on yourself, on other people, on the world, she learns to think and feel the same way. If you like who you are, are content with yourself and can celebrate your inner goodness (those energies of the heart I spoke of earlier), then she's more likely to enjoy herself too.

There isn't any external technique to modeling. You can't fake it. To model positive self-esteem you simply have to have it yourself. So if you don't, you might want to get working on that. (As a starter, I'd like to refer you to a mini-book I wrote called *Accepting Yourself,* published by JODA Communications, 1993.)

2. Quote what others say about your child.

Kids like to hear what others say about them. They often ask what so-and-so said. Quoting others is a form of indirection that allows you to send a message, but under the guise of it coming from someplace else. The only caution in quoting others is that you not lead a child to focusing his self-worth on the opinions of others.

To avoid this pitfall I quote others only when it involves a statement about my child's heart, not so much about behavior. Sometimes this is a tough distinction to make, but at least be aware that you're trying to send a message to your child about his inner self and not just about his behavior.

You go to your son's parent-teacher conference and get the scoop. When you get home, you let your son know his teacher likes the way he participates in class. "She said you bring a lot of energy to classroom discussions. I believe that. I see that at home too." Then let it go.

Your daughter's not doing well in spelling, but she tries hard. That's what you focus on and quote: "I know you're having some difficulty with spelling. But your teacher really praised your effort. She said you'd get it and she likes how hard you try. I like that too."

Other examples of quoting include:

"I saw Mrs. Wilson at the post office, and she said how much her children like it when you babysit for them. They think you're neat."

"Your coach said you are so eager to learn the game. She wished she had a whole team of kids like you."

"Grandma told me how much she appreciates it when you call her. She just loves you so much."

In this last example, saying "She just loves you so

much" is an indirect way of saying "I love you." Putting the words in somebody else's mouth is oftentimes much more powerful. Kids expect to be loved by you. So when others love them too it often registers more deeply.

3. Tell your child stories.

Stories reach the heart faster and more powerfully than any other form of communication. When you tell your child a story you put him in a hypnotic trance. Notice what happens to your child when you start telling a story. He focuses his attention on you completely. His breathing becomes more shallow. He doesn't swallow. He hardly blinks his eyes. He doesn't move a muscle. He's hypnotized. And in that hypnotic trance, the messages you send him go immediately to his subconscious mind and take hold. His subconscious mind applies the message of the story to whatever aspect of his life needs it. You don't have to make the point for him.

You can tell stories to teach any value you want. That's what the old morality plays were about. Tell a story to teach a value. In this case, the stories you want to tell have to do with teaching positive self-esteem. Narrating stories from your child's own life are often very effective in teaching personal worth. And they can be simple stories, examples or incidents in your child's life.

I tell my daughter, Amy, the story of how she had a high fever when she was one year old. It was the middle of the night and her fever wasn't going down. We needed to put her into a tub of cool water to reduce her fever. As

I began lowering her into the tub, the feel of the water was so cold, she began to cry and fuss. She fought, wiggled and scratched her way out of the tub. But she had to sit in there to reduce her fever. Her mom and I couldn't think of anything to do to get Amy to sit quietly in the tub. We brought in all her water toys. That didn't work. My wife read a story to her, hoping to distract her, while I tried to lower her into the tub without her even knowing it. Nothing worked. What to do?

Finally, I remembered the one thing that always worked with Amy—play with her. But in this case, to play with her meant I would have to get *into the tub with her.* Oh, my gosh! It was two o'clock in the morning on a cold night in December. At that moment I really didn't want to sit in a pool of cool water and play rubber ducky with my daughter.

But I did it. Oh, what love a father has for his daughter that he will sit in a tub of cool water on a winter night to help bring down her fever!

Once I was uncomfortably positioned in the tub, Amy happily joined me to play with boats, animals and soap. Her fever came down, and as the story goes, I got one heck of a cold.

This is a simple little story that told Amy I loved her, that she was worth my discomfort, that she was valuable enough for someone to extend himself to her in a caring way. At the end of telling her the story, I didn't need to explain the moral of the story. I didn't need to say: "Now, do you get the point of that story, namely that you are a lovable and worthwhile child?"

In fact, when you moralize you switch from right brain to left brain activity. You don't need to do that. Trust that her right brain will take in the information and make the application herself.

You can tell self-esteem stories about other people— make-believe or real.

I tell a true story of a young woman who went to graduate school with me and single-handedly stopped a violent demonstration at the University of Kansas during the time of the Vietnam War. This was a woman who believed in herself and in the cause of peace. She stood between the campus ROTC building and a couple of thousand students, challenging them to put down their rocks and sticks and seek peace through nonviolent means. She didn't care what they thought of her. She acted out of her own heart and her own beliefs.

That's a more dramatic story, but it gets at the same point of positive self-esteem and the need to believe in yourself rather than be taken in by the opinions and beliefs of others.

Oftentimes, parents tell me they don't have stories to tell. Oh, yes they do. They just haven't thought about them as stories of self-esteem. Spend some time with your partner or friend and talk about the things that have happened to you or to your child. As you talk of these things, you'll find examples and incidents that your child

loves to hear. And you will be sending great messages to
your child about self-worth.

4. Make background comments about events and people.

When my son, Andy, was very young, he'd watch
football games on television with me. During timeouts,
the army would advertise, recruiting young people to join
the service. The commercials looked very appealing,
telling youngsters they could join the army, get their
education, travel the world, and generally have a challenging and good time. I never liked those advertise-
ments and I didn't want my son buying that line. So I'd
sit back and toward the end of the commercial, I'd
comment: "Yeah, what they don't show you is the
caskets of the dead soldiers being carried off the planes."

I admit that was pretty strong stuff. But that's what I
did. Over the years, I'd drop in that comment every once
in a while during commercials for the military. I never
said anything else to my son about the army or those
commercials. Then one day when he was about 12 years
old, he and I were watching a sporting event on television
and a military commercial came on. At the end of it he
turned to me and said—as though he had never heard this
before in his life:

"Dad, you know, they never show the dead soldiers
being carried off the planes in caskets."

I replied, "That's a good point, Andy. Yeah, they
don't show that part, do they?"

You can send a lot of indirect messages to your children while watching television. You see someone acting in a caring way or in a cheery manner, and you can say in the background: "Now, there's a person who must like herself." You see someone training hard for a sporting event and say: "Boy, that takes a lot of determination and belief in himself to do that."

You can also do this in the car, at the dinner table or after seeing a movie. Just pay attention to what people are doing or saying, and then make an apparently off-handed remark that speaks of self-worth, inner strength or courage, personal belief over the opinions of others, self-care and enthusiasm for life.

For example, you might be eating supper and talking about your family's babysitter, who just went off to college. The kids like her and are talking about what she used to do with them and so on. At the end of the conversation, you might comment:

"Sarah is a young woman who really likes herself. That's neat."

That's all you need to say. Don't add to it: "And I hope you kids learn from her how important it is to like yourselves too." Please don't say that. Think, instead, that you are dropping little seeds of attitude into the gardens of your children's hearts. Your job is to plant. Let the nutrients of their own hearts and the waters of other people's love for them bring these attitudes and values to full bloom.

5. Talk to a third person so you're overheard by your child.

You're driving with a friend or spouse in the front seat and have your two little children in the back seat. They're talking and horsing around, while you and your front-seat passenger carry on a conversation of your own. All of a sudden, one of the children interrupts your conversation, asking, "Who was that? What did he do?"

Children hear what you're talking about even though they are engaged in their own activity. At least they hear bits and pieces of what you're discussing. Although they can appear totally involved in what they're doing, your words still play on the periphery of their awareness.

I'm sure you noticed that when your children were less than one year of age, a strange thing happened with television commercials. While playing with you on the floor, your child appeared to be totally unaware of the bowling game on television. That was just background noise for both of you. Neither one of you paid any attention to it. But as soon as the commercial came on, your child stopped what she was doing and watched the television set. Then when the commercial was over, she returned to her play. The commercials, with their brighter colors, upbeat sound and fast pace, grabbed your daughter's attention. All along she was taking in the background noise, but at certain moments she paid conscious and direct attention to it.

Children do the same thing with you. Your words and

actions often are background noise to them. (You knew that, didn't you!) At times, though, they pay direct attention to you. Either way, they hear your words and see your actions. They pick up, indirectly, your many messages about them, about yourself and other adults and children, and about life itself, even when you're not trying to send them any messages.

Why not make the background noise you create for your children work for them? When you're in the car talking to your partner or friend, throw in a comment occasionally about the neat kid in the back seat. The same at home, on the phone, with your neighbor. Do it about your neighbor's child as well. Feel free to spread the good news that these children are very good people. By telling it to another person, so your child overhears it, you send a powerful compliment, without the child being able to dismiss it in any way.

Often, a child who has low self-esteem rejects any comments made directly about what a good boy he is. He gets into an argument with you about not being a good boy. So send him your message indirectly by telling it to a friend or neighbor.

6. Tell your child positive things before and during sleep.

Sleep is a time when your child's unconscious mind works its miracles. What your daughter sees in her mind, what she thinks and feels before she falls asleep, tends to be carried to her unconscious mind and worked on through the night. The words you speak to her at this significant moment before sleep, I think, go a long way toward reinforcing self-esteem.

When you say goodnight, be sure you say "I love you." For many of you this instruction is obvious. But for others it is not. So be sure you say it. Also touch your child lovingly before she sleeps. Kiss her, hug her, smooth her hair. By doing so, you tell her you are with her, you love her because she is a lovable person.

You can tell her more. You can tell her she is a special child. She is unique (even if she doesn't understand that word), lovable and loving. You can tell her she's neat; you like being with her; and you're glad she's your daughter.

You can also send your child messages *while* she sleeps. Years ago I read an article about people under general anesthesia taking in the words of the physicians and nurses in an operating room. Despite their unconscious state they heard and recorded the conversations going on around them. If that is true, I thought, then perhaps my children would hear my words spoken to them while they slept.

So each night I went into Andy's room and said, "Andy, you are a lovable person. You are special and good. You are a loving, free boy who is trying to become his very best self. And I love you."

Then I'd go into Amy's bedroom and say, "Amy, you are a lovable person. You are special and good. You are a loving, free girl who is trying to become her very best self. And I love you."

No, they weren't transformed the next morning into highly energized, self-affirming children who only acted in loving and free ways. I don't know for sure if that exercise, repeated daily, had any direct effect on my children's self-esteem. I like to think that it did. Years later my children never said to me, "Dad, you know, I am a loving and free person who wants to be my very best self."

But even if this exercise by itself made no impact on them, it certainly made an impact on me. Because I spoke these words to my children every night, I came to believe them more and more profoundly as time went on. In part, because I said those words, they shaped my beliefs about my children. I came to firmly believe that my children are loving and free young people, who move toward being their very best selves. No matter what difficulties they have gotten into, no matter what decisions and judgments they have made, no matter where and how they have stumbled, underneath those behaviors there remain energies of their hearts that make them loving, free and striving-to-be-whole young people.

Telling them about their goodness every night allowed me to see beneath the surface of their lives to their hearts. And because I saw that goodness, I hoped that they too could see past their actions and the reactions of other people and accept themselves as good people.

Secretly, though, I actually believe they heard my words spoken with love every night when they were young. Now, of course, I no longer do that. My son is in college and my daughter goes to sleep later than I do. Perhaps she comes into my room now and whispers, "Dad, you are a loving and free man, who strives to become his very best self. And I love you." I'll have to ask her. Of course, she will look at me with a giant question mark on her face and then pronounce, "Dad, you're weird."

In teaching positive self-esteem to your children, indirection works better than direction. Try using the methods I've described. But a word of caution: Do not look for results immediately. You are planting tree seeds. Trees take a long time to grow. Think of yourself as a nursery owner—that is, a garden and tree nursery. You need tremendous patience and a long-range view. You plant the seed of the elm tree. You water it, fertilize it, weed around it. But it takes years before it really looks like an elm tree.

Self-esteem needs to be seeded and nurtured. The messages you send your children are the seeds and nutrients that work within the heart of each child. You don't see the workings of their hearts very clearly. But like the nursery worker, you need to believe that growth is taking place. With a tree sapling you can see growth. You can measure year to year how many inches the tree has matured. With your children, the measurements are much harder to make. You can't always see the growth of their hearts. But believe growth is taking place.

I have become optimistic about children and our ability to nurture their hearts. Once in a while I run into a young man or woman at a mall or a ball game who comes up to me, points a finger at me, and asks, "Aren't you a shrink?" After confirming my identity, we discover this young person was a client of mine 10 or 20 years earlier. At that time he was a teenager doing poorly in school. I always ask if he remembers our counseling, and happily the answer is usually "yes."

Then I ask the critical question, "Did you learn anything from that counseling?"

I am pleased to announce that the answer is almost always "yes" again. And the truly exciting thing to me is that the young man can tell me things he learned and things I said to him.

I always walk away from those brief encounters surprised and satisfied. I think back to when I worked with this young man and remember feeling frustrated and useless. I didn't think anything I said or did made it past the skin on his nose. Certainly I didn't think my words reached his heart.

But now I have changed my mind. When I work with young people I'm optimistic that my words will be incorporated and penetrate deeply into their minds and hearts. As the great psychotherapist and hypnotist Milton Erickson used to say to his clients, "My words will go with you." Your positive messages of self-worth will go with your children.

Gifting your children with high self-esteem overshadows everything else you do as a parent. You can teach your children to catch a ball, study for an exam, play the flute, tap dance, juggle, snuggle and do cartwheels, but all that stuff falls a distant second to gaining strong, confident feelings of self-worth.

Armed with a positive sense of self, your children will march into life secure, optimistic and happy. Able to say "yes" to themselves, they will walk with fearless energy, facing head on the challenges, the struggles and the delights of life. No matter what they do or what happens to them, deep down they will know their own goodness and value. No one and nothing will tear that sense from their hearts. They will always hear your voice, magnifying the voice of their own hearts: "You are a loving, free person who wants to be your very best self." Strong, wonderful self-esteem—that's your lasting gift, your inheritance to your children.

About the Author

Dale R. Olen, Ph.D., lives in Germantown, Wisconsin, with his wife, Joelyn, and their two children, Andy and Amy. Andy studies political science in college; Amy studies, works, and plays basketball in high school. They have a friendly beagle and an independent cat.

Dale received his doctorate in psychology from the University of Kansas in 1973. A year earlier he founded **The Justice and Peace Center** in Milwaukee, a social action organization attempting to create structural and societal change. During this time he realized that justice meant creating the opportunity for people to exercise their most basic right—namely, the right to live humanly. In his effort to understand what "living humanly" meant, he identified 14 "life skills" that fully alive people exhibit. He realized that his life's work was to help people develop these life skills so they could live full and happy lives. As a result, he started **Life Skills Center,** a mental health agency that he still directs today.

Dale teaches life skills through his writing, his lectures and workshops, and by doing psychotherapy. Since most people spend the majority of their time and energy at home and in work, he has concentrated his teaching in those two areas. He directs his life skills programs and materials toward families and businesses.

Dr. Olen is available for lectures and workshops.

Index

O R D E R   F O R M

TITLE OF BOOK	UNIT PRICE	QUANTITY	TOTAL
LIFE SKILLS PARENTING SERIES:			
Self-Esteem for Children	9.95		
Parenting for the First Time	8.95		
Thoughtful Art of Discipline	8.95		
LIFE SKILLS SERIES:	49.95 set of 10		
Accepting Yourself	5.95		
Thinking Reasonably	5.95		
Meeting Life Head On	5.95		
Managing Stress	5.95		
Communicating	5.95		
Being Intimate	5.95		
Reducing Anger	5.95		
Overcoming Fear	5.95		
Defeating Depression	5.95		
Resolving Conflict	5.95		
Add shipping and handling: 1–2 books $2.50; 3–5 books $4.50; 6–10 books $5.50			
Wisconsin residents add 5-1/2% sales tax			
		TOTAL	

M E T H O D   O F   P A Y M E N T

☐ Check enclosed (make payable to JODA Communications, Ltd.)
☐ VISA   ☐ MasterCard

Credit card #_____

Expires_____ Signature_____

Mail order form with payment to: JODA Communications, Ltd.
                        10125 West North Avenue, Milwaukee, WI 53226
Or call 414-475-1600. Please have your credit card information ready.
Please ship books to:

_____
Name

_____
Street Address

_____
City   State   Zip Code

_____
Phone

Other books by Dale Olen

LIFE SKILLS PARENTING SERIES:
Parenting for the First Time
The Thoughtful Art of Discipline

THE LIFE SKILLS SERIES:
Accepting Yourself
Thinking Reasonably
Meeting Life Head On
Managing Stress
Communicating
Being Intimate
Reducing Anger
Overcoming Fear
Defeating Depression
Resolving Conflict

649.1   O 45s

✓✗

SELF-ESTEEM

for

Chi

A pa

AFY 8686 -1

CH